HORNBY
magazine yearbook

Edited by Mike Wild

Contents

Cover: Bath Green Park was the worthy winner of *Hornby Magazine's* first Layout of the Year Competition in 2007. A Fowler '2P' 4-4-0 pilots a Bulleid 'West Country' 4-6-2 on departure from the evocatively modelled station. Chris Nevard.

Title page: A 'King Arthur' 4-6-0 crosses the road at Wellbridge, as modelled by the Crawley Model Railway Society. Chris Nevard.

Editor: Mike Wild **Designer:** Matt Chapman
Contributors: Chris Nevard, John Wiffen, Andrew Roden, Paul Appleton, Anthony New, Ian Morton, Paul Marshall-Potter, Ian Fleming, Keith Gordon and Katy Wild.

First published 2008

© Ian Allan Publishing 2008

Published by Ian Allan Publishing Ltd.

An imprint of Ian Allan Publishing Ltd, Hersham, Surrey KT12 4RG.

Printed in England by Ian Allan Publishing Ltd, Hersham, Surrey KT12 4TG

Visit the Ian Allan Publishing website at *www.ianallanpublishing.com*

ISBN 978 0 7110 3354 2

The past 18 months have been filled with new models, wonderful layouts and many new announcements. Tim Maddocks' Bleakhouse Road featured in HM July 2008 and showed just how appealing the Somerset levels are to the branch line modeller. Chris Nevard

Welcome

It seems like only yesterday that we were working on the first issue of *Hornby Magazine*, but in fact it is now 16 full issues since the first and now we're well on our way to publishing issue 17 as I write.

The first 18 months of this magazine's life have been a true whirl wind – they say time waits for no man, and that is certainly true of magazine publishing. As with any magazine we are driven by the industry which surrounds us and I'm happy to say that model railways are enjoying a buoyant time filled with exciting new releases, higher quality products than ever before and a greater range than many could expect.

This first *Hornby Magazine Yearbook* is a look back at the highlights of 2007 and 2008 including five favourite layouts chosen by readers through our first Layout of the Year Competition from 2007, the best track plans from Anthony New's series and a look back at the new models which shaped the past 18-months. But that's not all, as *Hornby Magazine's* contributors have been working hard to produce new material to whet your appetite for modelling, show you what's possible and explain that model railways don't have to be complicated. We're here to help modellers new and returning, make the most of this wonderful hobby and that is what the magazine will continue to do.

There genuinely has never been a better time to start. Digital Command Control has opened up a new field of opportunities while the range of models – whether you've a passion for the Western, Southern, Midland, Eastern Scottish Region – has never been better, even though there are still gaps to be filled. For diesel and electric modellers times are good too as Bachmann, Heljan and Hornby strive to develop ever better models, both locomotives and rolling stock.

The big story of 2007-2008 has to be the rapid development of 'N' gauge. Sure, it has been developing for a while now, but I think the last 12-months, with the release of the Bachmann Class 04 diesel shunter, LMS Stanier 'Jubilee', Class 37 and 'Warship' along with Dapol's 'Q1' and '9F' models have really shown just how much potential this scale holds. As a once long-term 'N' gauge modeller myself the attraction is back and, even though I'll be sticking with 'OO' gauge, the prospect of an 'N' gauge project layout is getting all the greater as more new models are announced and released.

As I've said this is buoyant time for the hobby and whichever scale you model in, or are considering, we're never had it so good. So, enjoy the *Hornby Magazine Yearbook*, but more importantly, enjoy the hobby, enjoy what we have and make the most of what the manufacturers are prepared to do for us.

Happy modelling!

Mike Wild
Editor, *Hornby Magazine*
Peterborough, August 2008

Bath Green Park

Hornby Magazine's layout of the year 2007

This spectacular model of Bath Green Park, the glorious terminus of the Somerset and Dorset route, was chosen by *Hornby Magazine* readers as their favourite of 2007. This is the how the Taunton Model Railway Group's layout caught their imagination. *Photography, Chris Nevard and Mike Wild.*

The station frontage has been beautifully modelled and has a wonderful atmosphere too.

The Somerset and Dorset Railway from Bath to Bournemouth is a railway like no other. This route, often referred to as the 'Slow and Dirty' – or S&D, was a regular haunt for legendary railway photographer Ivo Peters, whose images have left a timeless reminder of this much-lamented and greatly missed cross-country route.

The terminus of the S&D was Bath Green Park – opened on 4 August 1869 and originally named Bath Queen Square for the Midland Railway's extension from Mangotsfield. In 1874 the Somerset and Dorset Railway joined the Midland at Bath Junction and the two companies reached an agreement for joint use of the station.

In the post-1948 BR era this magnificent station echoed to the sounds of Midland and Southern locomotives as local trains shuffled onto the route and express trains, including the infamous 'Pines Express' arrived and turned to head to Bournemouth.

Previous page: Stanier 'Black Five' 44908 (a re-numbered Hornby model) simmers under the station roof at Bath Green Park after arrival with an inter-regional train. On the right an Ivatt '2MT' 2-6-2T draws to a halt with a local train.

The station itself was stunning, yet at the same time simple. It had just two platform faces, but it was the imposing trainshed over the four central tracks that gave the station its magnificent character together with the unmistakable clanking of ex-LMS locomotives appearing side-by-side with engines from the Southern Region.

Sadly the Somerset and Dorset Railway was hit by closure in the 1960s and in March 1966 the route closed altogether – four years after the last through train (the 'Pines Express' hauled by BR '9F' 2-10-0 92220 *Evening Star*) had traversed the line. Local traffic clung on, but it couldn't last forever. The Taunton Model Railway Group's recreation of Bath Green Park provides a lasting memory of this terminus station and captured the hearts and minds of Hornby Magazine's readers to become Hornby Magazines Layout of the Year 2007.

History of a model

The Taunton Model Railway Group began work on Bath Green Park 10

years ago. The idea was to produce a complimentary project to their existing layout, Tamerig Central, which is now permanently based at the TMRG's headquarters at Bishops Lydeard, and also create a new exhibition layout at the same time.

Modelling the jointly-worked Midland Railway and Somerset and Dorset Railway station at Bath, Somerset, seemed a reasonable proposition. It offered a double/single track junction, a goods yard, two engine sheds sharing a single turntable, siding loops and a sizeable two-platform terminus with a magnificent glass and iron main shed structure. Factors which influenced the final decision included the complexity of the challenge and the opportunity to run motive power and rolling stock design originating from all four post-1923 main line railway companies, and BR designs up to 1966.

From the outset, TMRG members aimed for the highest practical standards to create an accurate model of the prototype. Bath Green

Park offered sufficient individual projects for most of the group to become involved and better still, the prototype remained an unmodernised railway right up to its demise. From a modelling point of view the group was fortunate that the train shed and most of the original station buildings remain in use as part of a Sainsbury's supermarket complex in Bath.

"The project has required very considerable research. Track and building plans and many photographs have been kindly loaned for close examination. Even now, fresh information continues to appear. In one sense the layout can never be completed, but we assess about 95% has been achieved (or plans exist), for inclusion into our model."

Representing nationalisation

The period chosen represents the post-1948 BR years to 1966. As the railway was constantly developing and changing, not all features modelled existed simultaneously, it being impossible to obtain a fully comprehensive set of information recording a particular point in time.

"All the features portrayed are supported by evidence of accuracy within our chosen timespan. The vast majority are correct for the full period, but as every keen modeller will know, railway infrastructure is a constantly changing canvas of details," David said.

"The original station was a Victorian masterpiece built by the Midland Railway, which survived after its demise into the 1923 grouping until the rundown to eventual closure, which began in 1962. Some upper quadrant type signals and track layouts alterations, mainly in the engine sheds (features we have included) reflect the more obvious alterations.

"The major objective was to construct a layout capable of display away from our clubroom. This required a strong baseboard design without excessive weight, achieved by using mainly 9mm plywood with circular holes cut in the cross bearers."

To make the model suitable for 'home' and 'away' use some sections

3 With the 6.05pm local to Binegar behind, ex-LMS '1P' 0-4-4T 58086 prepares to shunt its stock into the departure platform.

4 The overall roof of Bath Green Park has been magnificently detailed with columns and iron work.

5 Double-headed trains were a common feature of the Somerset and Dorset and, more interestingly, combinations varied more than on any other route. An ex-LMS Fowler '2P' 4-4-0 pilots an ex-SR Bulleid 'West Country' 4-6-2 away from Bath Green Park in a classic combination of S&D motive power.

6 The junction where the Somerset and Dorset route diverges from the former Midland Railway will be remembered forever. An ex-LMS '4F' 0-6-0 rumbles down the gradient from the S&D with a van train towards Bath Green Park station while an ex-GWR '45XX' 2-6-2T waits patiently for its next duty.

are duplicated. Four baseboards comprise the station, goods yard, and engine sheds – these are portable and common to both the clubroom ('home') and exhibition ('away') versions. The rest has been built twice – one set is geographically correct, built in a more or less straight line to reflect the prototype and is portable for exhibitions, the other set is built to fit within the clubroom in a curve and is fixed. The clubroom version

connects into the 'Tamerig Central' layout.

The 'away' layout has an overall floor 'footprint' of about 70ft x 12ft. David takes up the story: "after being taken on its 'holidays', as we describe our commitment to do this), the experience revealed difficulties with both the overall size and operation of it. We received considerable praise for the high standards of construction and authenticity of the scene portrayed.

We also attracted initial criticism for the limited level of operations, although with each appearance this improved, but the reality had to be faced and learnt the hard way that what we had built was not a model railway, but a model of a railway – there is a difference between these two approaches to operating any model, especially this one.

"We learned that in creating an almost exact model of the prototype, we had failed to also offer

correct realism of train operation. It was not sufficient to run into and out of the terminal with no serious attempt to portray prototype practice.

"The prototype track layout had been created to handle the traffic pattern that ran on the S&D and Midland systems, although we had over simplified our operating interpretation of it. The prototype comprised five basic traffic flows – through expresses between the north and Bournemouth that reversed in the station; local S&D passengers between Bath and Mangotsfield/Bristol; through S&D route freights to/from the Midland routes, principally to/from the North Somerset coalfields; and terminating freight traffic from both the Midland and S&D routes into Bath goods yard and local private sidings.

"It made better sense to attempt a prototypical service sequence to portray this diversity, but it proved to be more difficult than first thought. The desired full timetable operation generated too high an activity demand within the existing electrical control limitations. Success came when another operator was introduced to work two new mini-panels created to ease the workload

on the 'junction' and 'loco' panel console operators.

"A model railway timetable for an end-to-end layout has to be planned within the limits imposed by model operation (we use handheld conventional analogue controllers) as each operator can normally only control one movement at a time, unlike prototype practice (or on circular model layouts) where a signalman/model operator can control simultaneous movements. The modern systems of individual

digital train control could help, but are beyond our present club and personal budgets.

"The solution that emerged, after much burning of the midnight oils, has been to rotate the former fiddle yard through 180 degrees (reducing the overall length of the model) and rebuild it into a transit yard with a 'balloon' reversing loop.

"This now allows trains to run in a continuous direction to/from the station and yards with a layover period in the transit yard. By

7 Goods traffic was a major part of Bath Green Park's traffic, particularly with coal coming from the North Somerset coalfields. A Stanier '8F' 2-8-0 waits for the signals to clear at the head of a coal train whilst on the left a Southern Railway built Maunsell 'N' 2-6-0 is held in the goods loops with a van train.

8 **The locomotive shed was a prominent feature both of Bath and the photographs of Ivo Peters – a cameraman with a strong association with the Somerset and Dorset route. Fowler '2P' 4-4-0s stand in the shed yard amongst the staff and clutter which go towards making this layout so special.**

rebuilding the model in this way, we have not touched the layout design configuration or its construction; retained the full scenic area as before, and, as a bonus, slightly extended it. The 'fiddle' part of the

operating sequence has been eliminated as has the fiddle yard operator to offset the additional mini-panel operator. We've gained improved reliability by eliminating the manual handling requirement;

simplified train operations to work in a uni-directional sequence via the 'balloon' loop; improved operator ability to communicate with each other by being closer together; improved the spectator interest with

9 **No model of the Somerset and Dorset Railway would be complete without one of the Fowler '7F' 2-8-0s – a class of locomotive which only saw service on the S&D. A kit built model of '7F' 53808 departs Bath Green Park with a passenger train.**

the mini-panels for shunting operations, and achieved an important reduction in the overall 'footprint'.

Operating 'Green Park'

"The timetable requires a minimum of 12 train formations, and 16 engines. In practice an adequate margin is also on hand as a back up and to offer spectator interest. At the station, all trains change engines, mainly provided by light engine workings to and from the sheds as per prototype practice.

"The timetable provides a continuing cycle of movement activity. The full sequence usually takes about one hour, although the timed schedule is 40 minutes – yet to be achieved!

"Train movements are controlled by numeric displays (controlled by the junction and panel operator) to progress the movement sequence. In the clubroom these are larger, easy to read units, permanently affixed to the walls; on the exhibition layout we use miniature displays. In the clubroom, final confirmation to drive a train is given by exchanging simplified block bell codes on in-house built block instruments; on the travelling layout (where background noise intrusion in exhibition halls can be a potential consideration) coloured lights are displayed on the miniature numeric panels to signify 'ok' to begin driving a train. Light engine and shunting movements are controlled locally.

"We use direct overhead lighting to illuminate the layout, fixed in the clubroom, and portable for exhibitions. In the clubroom the main room lighting is dimmed to emphasise

the layout presentation, at exhibitions this feature varies between locations. Lighting is provided under baseboards to illuminate the main control consoles.

End of the road

"The initial planning for Bath (Green Park) occupied two years while the necessary research was undertaken prior to beginning construction. The major requirements were – baseboard design and size, methods of support, and how to transport them to fit into one vehicle. Then came the wiring loom design for the considerable number of track sections. We chose full 'cab control' whereby each track section switch (with minor variations) can control anywhere on the layout. This has been modified with experience, but the concept is excellent and works well.

"The scenery backdrop also required considerable research and is often praised – including by people who have lived or still do alongside the line, and a select few who have recognised their properties. All members have contributed to a real team effort requiring considerable dedication and commitment. The jury is still out on "would we do it again?" – we very much doubt it! We are agreed the long journey and the results achieved have, without doubt, been very worth while".

📷 10 Bath Green Park shed is visited by a number of different locomotive classes of Midland, LMS, Southern and BR origins. In this view, from left, an ex-LMS Hughes-Fowler 'Crab' 2-6-0 and Stanier 'Black Five' 4-6-0, a BR '9F' 2-10-0 and a BR Sulzer Type 4 adorn the shed.

Bath Green Park stats	
Owner:	Taunton Model Railway Group
Builder:	Taunton Model Railway Group
Scale:	'OO'
Track:	Peco Code 75
Length:	70ft
Width:	12ft
Layout type:	Terminus-transit yard
Period:	1948-1966

Bath Green Park Track Diagram

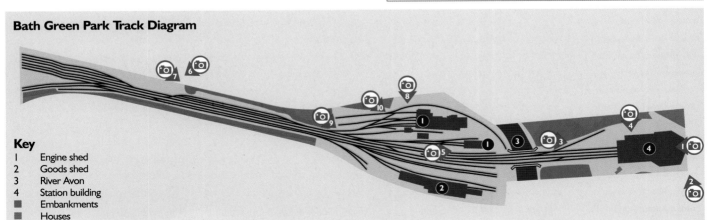

Key
1 Engine shed
2 Goods shed
3 River Avon
4 Station building
■ Embankments
■ Houses

So you want to build a model railway?

Starting a new project is always the hardest part, particularly when faced with a multitude of choices. PAUL APPLETON and MIKE WILD discuss the choices that lie ahead on the road to creating a world in miniature. *Illustrations: John Wiffen.*

Model railways are a wonderful pastime. They can take us back to a time of fond memories or allow us to follow our imagination. For the new modeller, with a blank canvas and the simple desire to build a working model railway it can be a minefield of choice. Should you start afresh with digital control, should you build a branch line or a main line and, perhaps most importantly, where will the layout be housed?

The answers to some of these questions will be easy. You might already have an allegiance to one BR region or another, or it might be that you have rediscovered an old box of Tri-ang Hornby models in the loft, sparking the flame and new ideas. A visit to a local model shop can be inspiring for a complete newcomer, but equally overwhelming.

In the past decade model railway technology has advanced immensely. Just a few years ago modellers

'made do' with coarse scale wheels and models which represented, not badly, but not perfectly, the locomotives which we treasure and enjoy. Today, technology has advanced to the point where computer aided design (CAD) and computer aided manufacturer (CAM) are all the rage and this has led to superb detailing, smooth running and reliable chassis and an overall quality of product that could hardly have been imagined just a few years ago.

Technology isn't just limited to the locomotives and rolling stock we have to choose from. Digital Command Control has revolutionised model railway operation, although conventional, or analogue control, hasn't disappeared by any means. Digital Command Control (DCC) has brought the opportunity for greater realism in terms of railway operation, but it has also added another choice to the potentially bewildering world of model railways.

There are countless stories of those who have started model railway projects that are destined never to be finished. Sometimes this is because of a lack of patience, or because the scheme they planned was simply too ambitious. It is important to get results reasonably quickly, otherwise it can be easy to be become disillusioned. The key is careful planning. Before rushing down to the local model shop to buy your first train set or buying those first sheets of timber, you need to consider a number of important factors. They may seem obvious at first, but you'll soon see the potential of this hobby.

The first question is not where to build a layout, or what scale. It is much more fundamental than that. The big question is why do you want to build a layout, really? It is important to answer this honestly, because in turn it will influence your

decisions on two other big questions. Just because you already have half a dozen 'OO' gauge locomotives, some lengths of track and an assortment of rolling stock, doesn't mean that you have to build an 'OO' layout. Let's face it, now's the time to change your mind before investing more money in, possibly, what could be the wrong scale.

Why build a model railway?
So, back to the question, why do you want to build a layout? Perhaps you want to see lots of trains running. Maybe it's driven by nostalgia – the chance to recreate childhood memories of your local railway or a main line which held your facination, or you're considering going as far as recreating a real railway location. Perhaps scenery is where you see the pleasure and you will enjoy seeing trains run through 'real' countryside. Or maybe it's railway operation – lots of sidings and shunting, or junction stations with branch lines.

But remember not to get carried away too soon. A balance is needed between operational interest and practicality. The simplest of layouts is based around a typical train set oval of track. This type of layout can be accommodated on a single 6ft x 4ft baseboard and offers a simple means to get trains running and start your enjoyment. Layouts of this style do have limitation in terms of realism,

so if this is your aim, it is worth considering one of the alternatives.

A simple style of layout is a portable or permanent end-to-end type. Typically this has a station at one end and a fiddle yard, where trains are stored, at the other. These are popular with those who like to exhibit at public events, because they are easy to transport and showcase their prized locomotives and carriages, but for a home-based layout, the operator can soon get tired by operational limitations.

However, small layouts do have their charms. For one it is much easier to see a small layout project through to completion. Similarly, it's also more cost effective and it can provide the basis to try out your skills before plunging into a much larger project. Compact layouts also lend themselves to detail, which is particularly good considering the impressive range of off-the-shelf buildings now available in the Hornby Skaledale and Bachmann Scenecraft ranges. If you're starting anew, then a small layout won't need

Major scales and gauges		
Name	Scale	Track gauge
Z	1mm:1ft	4.5mm
N	2mm:1ft	9mm
TT	3mm:1ft	12mm
HO	3.5mm:1ft	16.5mm
OO	4mm:1ft	16.5mm
O	7mm:1ft	32mm

Track gauges, their scales and actual widths.

John Wiffen.

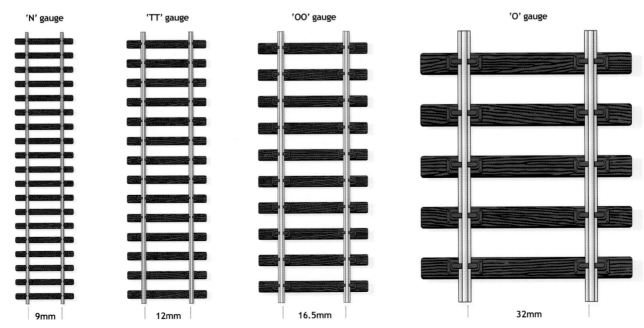

'N' gauge   'TT' gauge   'OO' gauge   'O' gauge

| 9mm | 12mm | 16.5mm | 32mm |

as much rolling stock to operate with, as there simply won't be the space. This also has the advantage that you can allow a collection to grow over time. Simple thoughts, but all worth considering.

Probably the most common home layout is a continuous run, or 'tail chaser'. These are layouts that go round in a continuous loop. They can be single or double-track main lines and generally provide more entertainment value than an end-to-end style layout. You might choose to include a large fiddle yard on one side so that trains can be changed after one circuit to add realism to the operation, or, if scenery is more important you could continue the main lines right round the room. Don't think though that you have to build an extensive layout for a continuous circuit. It could be as simple as a double track main line with a station and a couple of sidings on one side and a narrow fiddle yard on the other and in terms of size the continuous run can range from a train set style 6ft x 4ft baseboard to a massive 20ft plus layout built up of

a series of baseboards around the edge of a room. This way you may be able to accommodate two functions in the room which houses the finished model, such as storing a car in a garage.

Once you get beyond these two basic arrangements things start to get complicated; separate branch lines, junction stations, busy termini, split level lines, return loops and so forth. Don't worry if some of these terms don't mean much at this stage, they will be explained later, but suffice to say they would be a little ambitious for an absolute beginner.

A choice of scale

'OO' gauge, 4mm scale is the most popular in Britain. Gauge refers to the space between the rails, whereas scale is the proportion to a life-size 'one foot', meaning that 4mm scale is 4mm to one scale foot. The track is basically the same as that used in America and Europe for the slightly smaller 'HO' gauge (see table for details). In 'OO' there is far more equipment for the British market, including ready-to-run locomotives and rolling stock, buildings and accessories, than in any other scale.

Modern production techniques allow a high level of detail, but the

space needed to produce a realistic railway in miniature, with scale length trains and stations, gradual curves and correct large radius points would be enormous, especially where main line prototypes are concerned. For this reason most people who choose 'OO' build branch lines or cross country scenarios where train lengths are much shorter and the railway infrastructure more modest.

For example, if you want to run tender locomotives along a branchline, or into a seaside terminus for example, then it is not unreasonable to expect the station infrastructure to include a turntable and a servicing point or depot. This takes up quite a lot of room – at least 1ft (300mm) diameter for the turntable alone, so all of a sudden a lot of precious space is taken up. If you want to see full-length trains of more than six coaches, running through the countryside, or create a reasonable size town or seaside resort, 'N' gauge, 2mm scale should definitely be a consideration. Although this is 'half' the scale of 4mm, it actually takes up a quarter of the space, so much more track can be accommodated in a smaller area and the width of the baseboard takes up less track 'depth', allowing more space for scenery and buildings. For example, in a 2ft wide board you can get two full return curves in without them being too tight for trains to negotiate.

'N' gauge became something of a poor relation to its larger and more common counterpart, 'OO' gauge, until recently that is. Bachmann and Dapol are making tremendous strides in the quality of 'N' gauge models and where 'N' locomotives bore more of passing resemblance to their full size breathren, the latest models really are showing the true magic of this scale. In terms of performance, the quality of the mechanism inside the wonderfully engineered bodies now follows the standard we expect from the very latest 'OO' gauge models.

Few could have imagined that a highly detailed, fully motorised model of the tiny 200hp BR Class 04 diesel shunter would appear in 'N', but it has, and standards continue to rise. The variety of locomotives and rolling stock available in this small scale is also increasing to the point where it is well worth considering, particularly if you are short of space.

However, there are disadvantages to 'N' gauge – primarily the cost.

Rolling stock is comparatively more expensive, as most 'N' gauge models are priced in a similar bracket to the latest 'OO' gauge locomotives and rolling stock. But now, the quality is there and that is reflected in the price. Availability of equipment is no longer the problem it used to be, with Graham Farish now part of the Bachmann empire and Dapol producing an ever-growing range of locomotives and rolling stock in ready-to-run form. Even Hornby are now producing 'N' gauge buildings in their Lyddle End range (scaled down

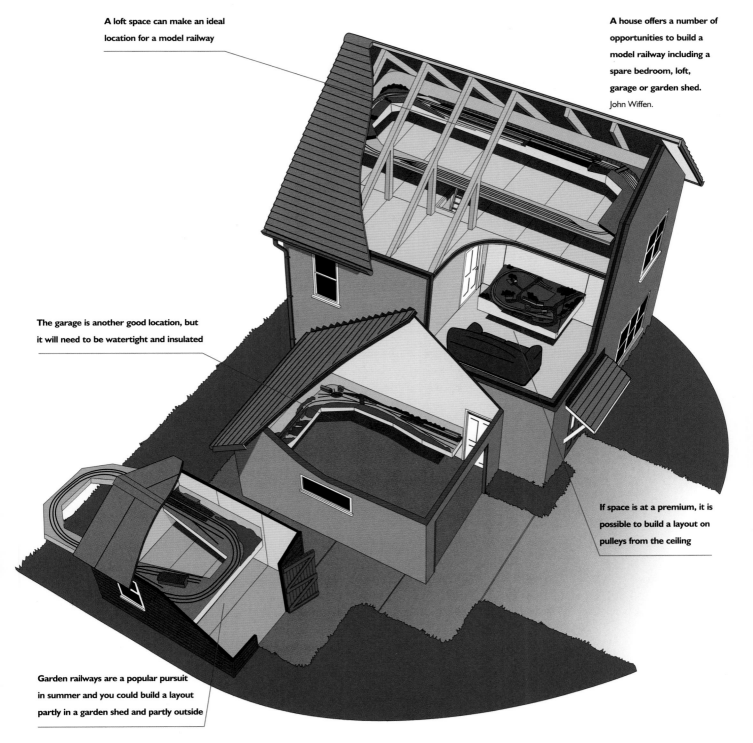

A loft space can make an ideal location for a model railway

A house offers a number of opportunities to build a model railway including a spare bedroom, loft, garage or garden shed.
John Wiffen.

The garage is another good location, but it will need to be watertight and insulated

If space is at a premium, it is possible to build a layout on pulleys from the ceiling

Garden railways are a popular pursuit in summer and you could build a layout partly in a garden shed and partly outside

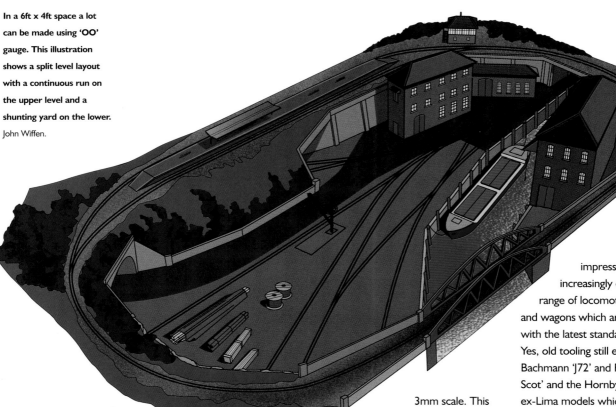

versions of the 'OO' gauge Skaledale buildings) and there are other manufacturers such as Peco who produce wagons as well as an extensive range of track and accessories and now a fully DCC fitted 'N' gauge model of the GWR Collett '2251' 0-6-0. There is also a superb range of kits for road vehicles goods wagons, locomotives and other scenic details which allow greater realism in 'N' gauge. Times have changed for 2mm scale and they are continuing to change with time. You only have to look at the new Bachmann Class 37 diesel and Stanier 'Jubilee' or Dapol's stunning 'Q1' 0-6-0 and 'M7' 0-4-4T to see that 'N' gauge is giving larger scales a run for their money.

A substantial layout can be produced in 'N' gauge and it can be a real solution if space is your limiting factor. There are some superb 'N' layouts doing the exhibition circuit and the N gauge Society caters for modellers of the scale and even produces its own range of wagon kits.

There is a scale/gauge between these two that many say is the perfect compromise: 'TT' gauge,

3mm scale. This allows a good compromise between space and detail considerations, but is not readily available in the shops. Tri-ang produced a reasonable range in the 1960s and you can still pick items up at swapmeets and toy fairs, but models are crude by today's standards and modellers in this scale need to be proficient in kit and scratchbuilding – that is to work with sheet materials, such as brass and plastic.

There is also a much smaller system than 'N' gauge, known as 'Z' gauge. This is tiny, and is really only of novelty value, particularly for the British modeller. There is little commercially available and what is, is of European outline. There are 'Z' gauge layouts on the exhibition circuit and there is no doubt that a huge amount of railway and scenery can be poured into a layout housed in the average size spare room – you can even build a basic layout in a businessman's brief case – but you can't really see what's going on, especially if you have eyesight problems!

Despite the improvements in 'N' gauge there is no doubt that 'OO' gauge remains a firm favourite which is in no small part due to the

impressive and increasingly comprehensive range of locomotives, carriages and wagons which are now available with the latest standards of detail. Yes, old tooling still exist such as the Bachmann 'J72' and Fowler 'Royal Scot' and the Hornby Class 86 and ex-Lima models which are now owned by Hornby – but none of these could ever be considered as a bad model. They still represent what they are supposed to and fill a small gap in the ready-to-run market which would otherwise be left unfulfilled.

As Hornby, Bachmann and latterly Heljan, the Danish firm, and new starter ViTrains have driven standards up with increasingly higher quality and more finely detailed models, so collectors and modellers have upgraded their fleets and sold off or part-exchanged their older, less sophisticated models, including earlier Hornby models and those from the now defunct Mainline and Airfix ranges. These older models are still pretty good, and someone starting out can get a number of locomotives or items of rolling stock for the price of just one new Hornby or Bachmann locomotive. But be sure to give them a thorough testing before committing to the purchase of a second-hand locomotive, or better still, find a dealer which sells pre-tested models

For the new starter on a budget, Hornby introduced a brand new range of models in September 2007 known as Railroad. This is a range of budget priced items which are based

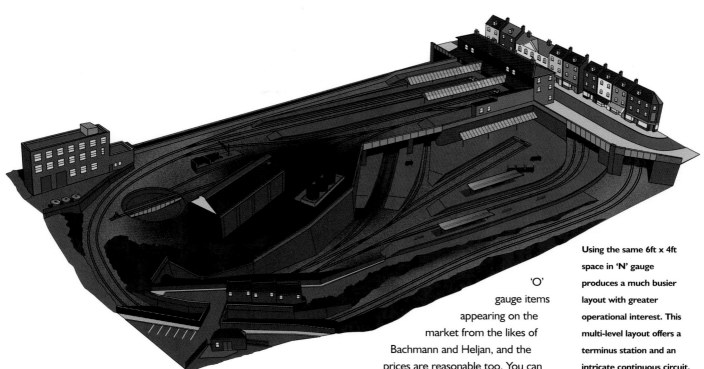

on earlier toolings and includes locomotives, coaches and wagons that the aforementioned new, upgraded items have replaced. Already available are 0-4-0T and 0-4-0ST shunting locomotives, a locomotive powered model of the famous Gresley 'A3' 4-6-2 4472 *Flying Scotsman*, Pullman carriages and open wagons. During 2008 Hornby will be adding a budget model of the streamlined Gresley 'A4' class 'Pacific' and the BR '9F' 2-10-0. Railroad's prices start from just £20 for a locomotive, which is stunning value considering the quality and smooth running characteristics of the samples tested in the *Hornby Magazine* office.

Going large...

If you really want a lot of fine detail then you can always look at going bigger than 'OO'. There are finer scale variations of 'OO' such as 'EM' and 'P4' which are really for those who seek perfection, but 'O' gauge, 7mm scale, achieves another level of realism altogether. With 32mm between the rails, locomotives in this scale dwarf those in 'OO' with dimensions that are almost four times the size.

Of course the biggest problem here is finding the space. 'O' gauge

layouts look great, but for most people they simply aren't practical. Typically you need at least 12ft for a basic end-to-end layout. You might just have room for a simple station with one platform and a run-round loop and, maybe a couple of sidings. There won't be room for a traditional fiddle yard to store trains, so a cassette system or traverser will be required to avoid the need for points leading to the sidings. Building this sort of system can again be daunting for the beginner.

Usually, 'O' gauge is something that seasoned modellers progress to as most locomotives, coaches and wagons need to be built from kits, although there is an increasing number of ready-to-run

'O' gauge items appearing on the market from the likes of Bachmann and Heljan, and the prices are reasonable too. You can pick up a fully operational locomotive now for under £300, but even at these prices you are unlikely to have a large fleet.

To utilise 'O' gauge at its best you need a big room, like a double garage, or perhaps a garden. Yes, you can safely run 'O' gauge, and indeed 'OO', in the garden, but the most popular choice for garden railways is one called 'G' scale.

'G' scale is something of a misnomer really, because although the track is a constant gauge, the scale depends upon the size and type of train that you choose to run on it. With 'G' scale you can run German outline stock from LGB which is based on

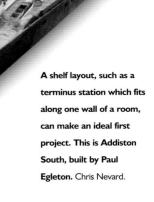

A large layout like Kirkby Stephen West, which measures 22ft x 10ft, offers scope for scenic modelling. This 'OO' layout was built by two members of the Huddersfield Railway Modellers and is modelled on the real Kirkby Stephen West station on the Settle & Carlisle line. Mike Wild.

real life metre gauge trains on the same track as British outline standard gauge, so this means that scales are something quite different.

It starts to get complicated here, but there are so many permutations across the scales and gauges, such as running narrow gauge trains on 'OO' track or narrow gauge trains in 4mm scale which run on 'OO9' track – 9mm gauge track – that we've added a separate section to this book all about the different scales and gauges there are to choose from.

There are also in-between scales that we haven't mentioned, such as 'S' gauge, but because of the lack of ready-to-run equipment it has to be scratch built, which is beyond the capabilities of most of us, at least for now. In the garden there are larger scales still, including Gauge 1 and on into what are known as miniature railways, capable of hauling passengers, and almost always live steam. Live steam is generally only used from 'G' Scale upwards, but there are exceptions and many of you

will be aware of Hornby's remarkable 'OO' gauge live steam system where model locomotives are powered by a single cylinder hidden beneath the body feed by a small 'immersion' heater located in the tender. Wonderful stuff and great fun to operate.

Location, location, location...
So let's think about it. What space do you have available? If you do want a substantial 'OO' layout you may have to consider options outside of the home. But first, let's look inside the home, for undoubtedly this is the best place for a model railway due to the consistency of temperature and ease of access.

A spare bedroom is perfect. Options here include having a railway running round the outside wall, either all the way round in a continuous run or in part, such as an 'L' shape or end-to-end. Building a railway around the edge of the room can make it multi-functional too, so you can share the space with another's hobby too. 'N' gauge will allow the use of one side of the room, even for a continuous run,

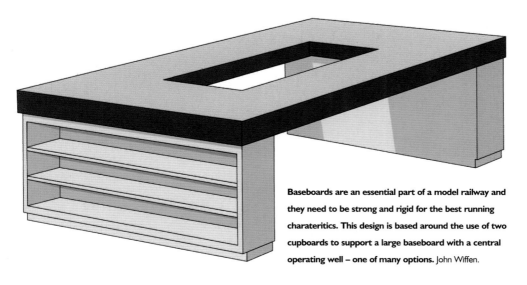

Baseboards are an essential part of a model railway and they need to be strong and rigid for the best running charateritics. This design is based around the use of two cupboards to support a large baseboard with a central operating well – one of many options. John Wiffen.

allowing easier access to the room and a clear operating area. If the room is big enough, you might consider a layout built in the middle of the room so you can get around it easily.

If you haven't got a spare room then don't worry, there are ingenious ways of concealing a railway in the guest room, or any other room for that matter. For example, you can have one that lowers down from the ceiling using pulleys or you can have one which folds up against the wall on hinges. A portable layout can be designed to fold away or split into sections and be stored in a cupboard or under the bed when not in use. The permutations are only limited by your imagination.

Next best after the house itself is perhaps the garage, but beware of drafts, the damp, and creepy-crawlies. The best bet is to empty it and line it with timber and replace up and over doors with something more conventional that will keep drafts at bay. A good electrical supply will also be required, as well as good lighting and you may need to consider resurfacing the concrete floor. But converted garages do give a good deal of space. They can also be used even when the garage is still required for the family car, using the aforementioned fold down or hoist-from-ceiling methods.

Given the right kind of building, the loft can make a superb model railway room. More modern homes have a criss-cross system of trusses and beams and aren't practical for conversion. But older buildings, and especially bungalows, have good open spaces that can be utilised. Lofts are draughty and need to be in order to keep air circulating and avoid damp. However, they are also prone to extreme temperature changes from winter to summer. Velux windows and heating systems can get round this to some extent, but it can still be extremely uncomfortable in the height of the summer and trackwork can suffer due to expansion in extreme conditions.

Another disadvantage of using the loft is the cost involved in converting

it, not to mention clambering up and down to it. You will need a professional electrician to add a power supply and good lighting.

If none of the locations discussed so far are appropriate then we are really talking about moving into the garden. A purpose-built shed is an option. A substantial shed of 12ft x 8ft would allow for a decent layout in either 'N' or 'OO'. As well as the initial cost of the structure and building it yourself, or paying someone else to build it, you will also need to insulate it and line it with a second wall of timber or plasterboard. The floor will need extra insulation to stop the cold and damp from coming through and the roof will need to be thoroughly waterproofed and lined. An electrical supply will also need to be laid from the house by a qualified electrician.

The main disadvantage though, apart from venturing out in wet weather, is security. A garden shed will always be vulnerable to burglary however many locks and bolts you attach to the door.

Other than the shed, there is the garden, but this is a very different sort of proposition. Buildings and structures need to be weatherproof or portable and intricate trackwork isn't always suitable. Outdoor layouts in 'OO' are great for watching scale length trains go by, but there are operational limitations of a very

different kind and winter running is almost impossible, although we have seen 'G' Scale layouts operating in the snow!

No space? Join a club...
For most beginners there is an option amongst this lot, but if none of these are for you, there is another possibility: use someone else's layout! Yes, I am being serious. There are two prime options. First, consider joining your local model railway club.

Most clubs have at least one layout in the principal scales under construction or operational and you will be welcomed with open arms. You can gain useful tips from fellow members and learn new skills on club nights. You will be able to run your own locomotives and rolling stock during club running sessions and perhaps at exhibitions when the club layout is invited to attend.

The second option is to team up with a friend who has more space at home than you have. Working with someone else can be good fun and you can learn to solve problems together. Furthermore, larger layouts usually need more than one operator to get maximum enjoyment and use.

So there are no excuses, whether you dust off those old Tri-ang Hornby models from the loft or are about to start out afresh, hopefully the options discussed here will inspire you to get started.

The scenic section of this layout is only 3ft x 2ft 6in, and offers a single platform station and a small shunting yard in a compact space. A pair of 2ft long cassette fiddle yards complete the 7ft long layout. Mike Wild.

'O' gauge/7mm scale

'OO' gauge/4mm scale

Gauging the right scale

Choosing the best scale to model in can be a tricky decision. ANDREW RODEN explains the popular scales, and how well supported they are.

Of all the questions facing someone about to start railway modelling, perhaps the most fundamental is that of which scale to choose. There is a bewildering array of possibilities and reasons to choose, or not choose, any one – and that's why we're publishing this guide.

For most of us, it comes down to a compromise between the space we have available; as opposed to the space we'd like to have! We also have to consider whether our chosen prototypes are available in that scale, what it is we want to model, affordability, and our own modelling skills. For example, we might want to fit an

'O' gauge, 7mm scale, main line in a box room and run 15-coach expresses, but practical considerations of space and price mean, in that case, a smaller scale would be better.

It's worth clarifying scales and gauges briefly. Many modelling magazines, Hornby Magazine included, use them interchangeably when talking about models. For the most part, this makes no difference as when something already built is being discussed, there's little scope for confusion. However, when we're talking about the range of different scales, it can make a huge difference. 'Scale' is the ratio of the model to real life, usually expressed in millimetres to the foot or as a

proportion. 'Gauge' is the distance between the rails, and can be independent of the scale. Standard Gauge is 4ft 8½in in the real world, and many scales reflect this. However, not all model standard gauge accurately, and when it comes to modelling narrow gauge railways, such as those in Wales, a completely different track gauge is used instead. For our purposes, titles such as 'N' or 'OO' scales refer to the popular names for those combinations of scale and gauge.

There's no right or wrong in railway modelling, so if you're still deciding which scale to model in, here's our guide to the various scales and gauges.

The main scales are 'N', 'OO' and 'O' gauge. These locomotives show a comparison between the three. John Wiffen.

'N' gauge/2mm scale

in the 1960s under the 'TT' (or 'table top') banner, 'TT' has long been viewed as an ideal compromise between the small-size of 'N' and the more detailed, but larger 'OO' models. Despite its seeming advantages, it remains a minority scale with few if any ready-to-run models. Kits are available of a fair range of prototypes, and there is healthy support in the shape of the 3mm Society.

'HO'
Scale: 3.5mm: 1ft
Gauge: 16.5mm
Notes: The first popular miniature scale, 'HO' is by far the world's most popular, and is exactly half the scale of 'O'. A huge amount of track and scenic products is available from a massive number of manufacturers, but very few British models have been produced, thanks to the dominance of 'OO' and the limited possibilities of operating British models alongside their continental counterparts.

'Z'
Scale: 1.38mm: 1ft
Gauge: 6.5mm
Notes: The smallest mass-produced scale, 'Z' offers the potential to build truly tiny layouts crammed with detail. For British modellers it is something of an irrelevance as few UK-outline models have been produced, but if space is at an absolute minimum, continental models are available, although at a price.

'N'
Scale: 2mm: 1ft
Gauge: 9mm
Notes: After many years as the poor relation to larger-scale models, recent releases in 'N' are finally showing the potential of this scale. There is a wide and growing range of British models, mainly produced by Bachmann under the Graham Farish banner, and Dapol. A comprehensive range of track and scenic products is available including ready-made buildings from Bachmann's Scenecraft

and Hornby's Lyddle End range, and the small size of the models means a miniature main line is a genuine possibility even in comparatively small rooms.

'TT' (also known as 3mm)
Scale: 3mm: 1ft
Gauge: 12mm
Notes: First popularised by Triang

'OO'
Scale: 4mm: 1ft
Gauge: 16.5mm
Notes: The most popular British scale, 'OO' started out as a compromise before the Second World War as it wasn't felt possible to motorise British outline models in 3.5mm: 1ft 'HO' scale due to the

Narrow gauge modelling has a charm all of its own. This 'OO-9' layout, Ditton Heath built by John Thorne, shows just how much can be achieved with creativity and an open mind.
Chris Nevard.

'OO' gauge is undoubtedly the most popular, particularly as it has the largest support from ready-to-run manufacturers. This is Hinton Parva, built by the High Wycombe and District Model Railway Society. Chris Nevard.

Other scales

There are other scales that attract modellers. To begin with, there are finescale equivalents of 'N' (2mm finescale) and 'OO' (Protofour, sometimes known as 'P4'). Both of these scales are built to extreme levels of accuracy, with track and rolling stock almost invariably having to be built from kits or from scratch. Some fabulous models in both scales have been built, but the attention to detail demanded of them means they tend to be for the most dedicated modellers.

Other niche scales include 'S' (4.76mm: 1ft with 22.2mm track gauge), and in narrow gauge, 'G', which uses 45mm gauge track, but whose scale is entirely up to the modeller! In this latter scale, most scratchbuild, often with the aim of running live steam locomotives, but there are also a number of ready-to-run models for this scale including LGB and Bachmann Aristocraft products. There are others still, including finescale and 'coarse' variants of 'O' and Gauge 1, and if you're prepared to build your own track, a myriad of narrow gauges. The choice is yours…

smaller size British prototypes. The result is that the track gauge – exactly the same as 'HO' – is incorrect, and looks it. Nonetheless, there are ready-to-run models and kits of many prototypes – locomotives, carriages, and wagons – and excellent support from the manufacturers. Accurate models of real locations can take a huge amount of space, but

most homes have the space for a decent 'OO' scale layout.

'EM'
Scale: 4mm: 1ft
Gauge: 18mm
Notes: 'EM' uses 'OO' models re-gauged to a more accurate track gauge of 18mm, and the track work looks far better than the extra 1.5mm between the rails might initially suggest. Re-wheeling carriages and wagons is fairly easy, but locomotives, particularly steam, can be daunting. However, for those with the time and patience, a good layout is perfectly possible. Flexible track can be bought, but points and other trackwork will need to be built from scratch. Support is provided by the EM Gauge Society.

'O'
Scale: 7mm: 1ft
Gauge: 32mm
Notes: The first railway models available to the masses, the heyday of 'O' was arguably between the wars, when there was little alternative. Since then the scale has

waned in popularity, despite the presence and detail of current models. Space and affordability are the two main deterring factors for many, though some excellent 'O' scale models have been built in very small spaces. Many find building kits and scenery easier in 'O' because of the larger scale, and there is a good range of track and kits available, as well as some ready-to-run models including more recently those from Bachmann Brassworks, Heljan and a handful of specialist builders. Live steam models provide a chance to drive real engines, and the scale is particularly suited for gardens. The Gauge O Guild has over 5,500 members.

'Gauge 1'
Scale: 10mm: 1ft
Gauge: 45mm
Notes: Another large scale, 'Gauge 1' is about the largest practical for most. At this end of the spectrum, models are really big and heavy, and with price tags to match. Battery and electric power supplies are all used, but for many 'Gauge 1'

modellers, the possibility of running real steam is a major attraction. Many locomotives are powered by gas or liquid fuel, but some burn coal. If you have the space and money, a 'Gauge 1' layout is as close to a 12in: 1ft prototype in the back garden as you'll ever get!

Narrow Gauges
There are lots of narrow gauge railways around the world and in Britain, and by using a smaller track gauge than the standard gauge equivalent in a given scale, narrow gauge layouts are fairly straightforward to build, and often have a lot of character that main line railways could never match. Many choose to invent their own railways rather than follow a prototype, giving full vent to a modeller's creativity. Here is a brief round-up of some of the possibilities.

'N-6.5'
Scale: 2mm: 1ft
Gauge: 6.5mm ('Z' gauge)
Notes: Using 'Z' track with 'N' scale models, 'N-6.5' offers a scale gauge of 3ft 3ins between the rails – roughly equivalent to metre gauge in real terms. At this size, modelling the Isle of Man railways wouldn't be an unreasonable compromise, and nor would the 3ft gauge Southwold Railway.

'OO-9'
Scale: 4mm: 1ft
Gauge: 9mm ('N' gauge)
Notes: One of the most popular narrow gauge scales, 'OO-9' equates to a gauge of 2ft 3in, making it ideal for models of many British narrow gauge railways, including the Talyllyn and Corris (which are spot-on gauge-wise), Welshpool & Llanfair, and with small compromises for gauge, the Ffestiniog, Welsh Highland, Vale of Rheidol, and Lynton & Barnstaple railways. 'OO-9' effectively uses 'N' gauge track with 'OO' scale models and, like 'OO', is modelled to 4mm scale. A good range of track and components is available, and while

most rolling stock is in kit form, many of the locomotives use standard 'N' gauge chassis, making that most difficult of tasks easier. The wide range of 4mm scale scenic components and buildings makes a layout very feasible.

'O-16.5'
Scale: 7mm: 1ft
Gauge: 16.5mm
Notes: With a similar range of

possibilities to 'OO-9' as far as prototypes is concerned, perhaps the main attraction of 'O-16.5' is that it allows 7mm: 1ft models to be used in much smaller spaces than their standard gauge equivalents.

Use of 'OO' scale chassis makes locomotives fairly straightforward, while the large scale means that a vast amount of detail can be included on layouts.

'N' gauge is becoming popular again now that Bachmann and Dapol are producing high quality ready-to-run locomotives and rolling stock. This is Oxbury Town, built by Carl Woodwards, and shows just how much can be compacted into a relatively small space in 'N'. Mike Wild.

Newport & Baconsthorpe

A small lottery win gave Alistair Durham the opportunity to recreate a small slice of the North West in the transition period of the 1960s. His layout came second in *Hornby Magazine's* first layout of the year competition so we revisit this now dismantled layout.
Photography, Mike Wild.

The North West of England is a popular choice for modellers, and none less so than Alistair Durham. His layout, Newport and Baconsthorpe, is firmly set in the transition period of the 1960s when steam was giving way to diesel traction in the North West and features both a low-level continuous run main line and an upper level branch line which runs from 'Newport' to 'Baconsthorpe' – the truncated terminus of the fictitious branch line.

Alistair takes up the story: "The railway bug first bit me when I was very young, probably in the early 1960s. We lived alongside the Coventry to London main line and through the 1960s I witnessed the disappearing steam scene, dieselisation and electrification. Add to this my Scottish auntie and uncle living close to the East Coast mainline near Dundee and, well, the rest is understandable history."

Like so many, Alistair had held onto his dream to build a model railway, but several factors held him back. Firstly he couldn't decide where to base the layout on and, in his own words: "Certain tasks also scared me off, like electrics and the time required."

Around 10 years ago, Alistair took the plunge after a small lottery win, not enough to retire on, but enough to pursue his layout plan, came his way and contacted Mike Thornhill of Kenwater Railways.

Planning permission granted

"The household authorities granted me planning permission and approved the budget and we were all set," Alistair added. "The layout was to be located in the rear bedroom and loosely based on somewhere near the coast in North West England, with interlopers from other regions to the local football ground and docks."

Despite being allocated a spare bedroom, space was still at a premium. In total the room offered 10ft 8in x 9ft 10in, which meant that a main line station wouldn't fit especially considering that long trains would be needed to create the right illusion. One of the aims was to create a layout where he could enjoy passing trains as well as shunting and general railway operation. The result was to develop a two-level layout which offers a continuous circuit on the lower connected to hidden storage loops so that trains can be changed over easily and a branchline running on a higher level. However, the fiddle yard hasn't proved to be the greatest design, but it works and trains have run from it for several years.

To get the project off the ground, Alistair turned to Mike Thornhill for assistance with the baseboards. Mike's services were also used to lay the track and install the wiring "The layout is what I describe as 'analogue' in so far as I have yet to go digital," Alistair said. "There are two operating panels, low level main lines and high level branch. These are hard-wired and points are operated by Peco motors via a pencil probe. Track cleaning is via Relco units. The whole operation is very robust and testament to Mike's skills: it has rarely, if ever, broken down aside from the odd failed point."

While the track work and electrics were tackled by Mike, Alistair concentrated his efforts on the scenic side of the layout. Commenting on the scenery Alistair said: "My contribution came with structures, scenery and endless painting of rails in rust colour! I have to say that I am really quite proud of the finished scenics, a first attempt at that and a lot of trial and error."

Fictional location

Like so many model railways, Newport and Baconsthorpe aren't based on real locations at all. The track plan, town, village, and even the football ground, are entirely fictional, but to confuse matters, there is a real village called Baconsthorpe in Norfolk.

The lower level main lines, double track with additional junctions, disappear into a tunnel complex serving Newport Central after passing the large stand of Newport Town Football Club. The branch to Baconsthorpe is served by the ex-LNER station at Newport Quay – a simple affair which requires a shunt release locomotive as there is no run-round loop. Completing the fictional tale, Alistair adds: "During the war, a connection was squeezed in from the approach/exit of Newport Quay to the ex-LMS mainlines. This was to facilitate moving ammunition to nearby army and RAF bases, the latter still being in use at Baconsthorpe."

As for time period, Newport and Baconsthorpe is firmly set in the 1960s, the period which inspired Alistair and the trains are hauled by steam locomotives in dirty, grimy condition alongside newer diesels. A good touch, depending how you look at it, is the row of withdrawn steam locomotives stored in a siding awaiting their fate at a breakers

3 The boiler house captures the dereliction of the 1960s as a Stanier 'Black Five' 4-6-0 – a Hornby model – passes with a goods train.

4 Steam is a rare visitor to the Baconsthorpe branch now that DMUs have been introduced. An Ivatt '2MT' 2-6-2T runs round its train before returning to Newport.

5 ▸ Right: Coated in soot and grime, BR '9F' 2-10-0 92199 emerges from the tunnel under the branch line with a heavy coal train.

6 ▸ Below right: At Baconsthorpe station, a Scammell Mechanical Horse waits for its load to be removed outside the goods shed.

7 ▸ Below: With a row of withdrawn steam locomotives dominating the background, a Hornby 'Black Five' rumbles along the main lines with a freight. Soon it will be replaced by diesel traction too.

yard. In general, dereliction is creeping in all around, although modernisation is on the horizon.

However, Newport Quay is a more modern station building, as Alistair says: "Newport Quay and docks were bombed in the Second World War and the station building was rebuilt very basically in the 1950s with a single storey replacement. In the fictional model world, plans are afoot to close Newport Quay, and all services will be diverted into Newport Central. By the late 1960s only a DMU service survives along with some freight, principally to RAF/MOD Baconsthorpe."

Motive power and services

Representing the North West in the 1960s means that Alistair has assembled a fleet of ex-LMS and BR steam locomotives, plus a selection of early diesel classes. Alistair takes up the story: "Traffic on the ex-LMS lines is hauled by BR '9F' 2-10-0s, ex-LMS 'Black Five' 4-6-0s, and '8F' 2-8-0s along with the occasional BR

'Britannia' class 'Pacific' or ex-LMS 'Jubilee'. Diesel classes vary from English Electric Type 1s and 4s, Type 2 diesels and Brush Type 4s: TOPS codes such as Class 20 don't – and probably never will – appear here!

"A 'Jinty' or two cling onto shunting duties although diesels are set to replace all shunting duties in late 1966. The branch line is virtually dieselised with Type 2s and DMUs, although occasional Ivatt 2-6-2T supplements when required or replace those failed diesels. The local football team is in the old Division 2 and as such match days have seen 'Warship' diesels, English Electric Type 3s, a 'Hall' and even a Blue Pullman set turn up at Newport Central! Local spotters have also noted an ex-LNER 'B1' 4-6-0, 'WD' 2-8-0 and an ex-LNER 'K3' visiting the docks with inter-regional freights."

The majority of the fleet is weathered, but rather than risk adding dirt and grime himself, Alistair has acquired several professionally weathered

8 An ice-cream van pauses outside the terraced houses as a Fowler 'Crab' 2-6-0 passes by in the background. Newport Football Club's stand dominates the skyline.

📷9 **The branch line to Baconsthorpe is now dominated by diesel traction, although steam does appear from time-to-time. A BR Sulzer Type 2 tackles the gradient from Newport on the branch to Baconsthorpe.**

locomotives from Ebay. Alistair commented: "All have run well and the weathering is generally excellent. Other factory-weathered locomotives have had weathering and detailing increased by myself. Really it is simply a matter of time and the fact that I really want to enjoy the hobby in that time.

"Passenger rolling stock is a combination of all regions: ex-LMS, LNER and Southern with Mk 1 coaches and the occasional early Mk 2, some being in the new

corporate blue and grey colour scheme rather than British Railways maroon. I remember stock really being a hotchpotch in the '60s and it was reasonably common to see maroon, blue and grey and green all mixed up. Indeed I saw Southern green coaches in Dundee regularly, presumably on cross-country workings. One can often see each period modelled, but rarely that blue/grey transition era.

"Freights consist of much coal and general goods traffic to the

docks or transferring for the docks. This is an element I would also like to expand on given the chance, by increasing the sidings and shunting movements.

The Future

Alistair hasn't stopped working on Newport and Baconsthorpe just yet though, and many will argue that no layout is ever complete. There is always another locomotive, a building, a road vehicle or some other detail which could, or sometimes should be added.

However, circumstances have now changed for the layout. "By the time you read this, Newport and Baconsthorpe will be no more as we will have moved to a new house just outside Evesham. The layout has been built in sections and has been dismantled and stored securely in the loft. I will be ensuring that the whole layout is removed by myself and not the removals men – I know who to blame then if things go wrong!

📷10 **The goods shed alongside the main line is kept busy with parcels and goods changing transport modes.**

"Sadly the bad news is that the new bungalow only has two bedrooms, but the good news is that it has a 40ft loft and a 33ft garage. I will rebuild, and I am hoping to salvage the branch and sections of the main line and of course the storage trackwork and most scenics and structures. If all goes as planned, this will be incorporated into a much longer layout, as I have always wanted to run near prototypical train lengths.

"Sometime in the future I will be able to relate to you all the nightmare of moving house and expanding the layout: wish me luck!"

Newport and Baconsthorpe statistics	
Owner:	Alistair Durham
Builders:	Alistair Durham and Mike Thornhill
Scale:	'OO'
Track:	Peco Code 75
Length:	10ft 8in
Width:	9ft 10in
Period:	1960s BR, North West

Newport and Baconsthorpe Track Diagram
Each square represents 1 square foot. Not to scale

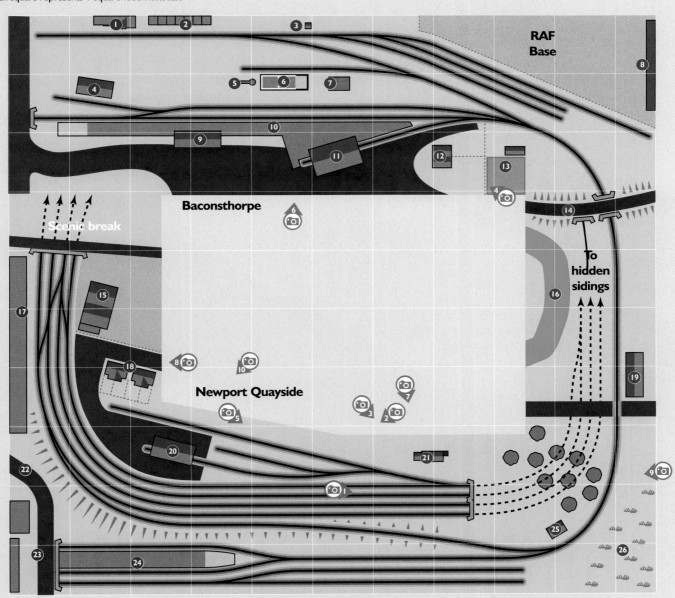

Key

1	School	9	Station building	18	Cottages
2	Cottages	10	Platform	19	Barnhill halt
3	Gate house	11	Goods shed	20	Goods shed
4	Provender store	12	Cottages	21	Derelict factory
5	Crane	13	Bowling green	22	Entrance to goods depot
6	Cattle dock	14	Abandoned line	23	Newport station
7	Water tower	15	Bus garage	24	Platform
8	RAF base and hangar	16	River	25	Station box
		17	Football stand	26	Marsh

Hornby Magazine's Top Ten trackplans

Layout planning is a complex subject which takes a lot of thought and preparation. Drawing on the high quality project ideas from Anthony New's series of layout plan articles, *Hornby Magazine* Editor MIKE WILD picks 10 of the best and highlights their potential.

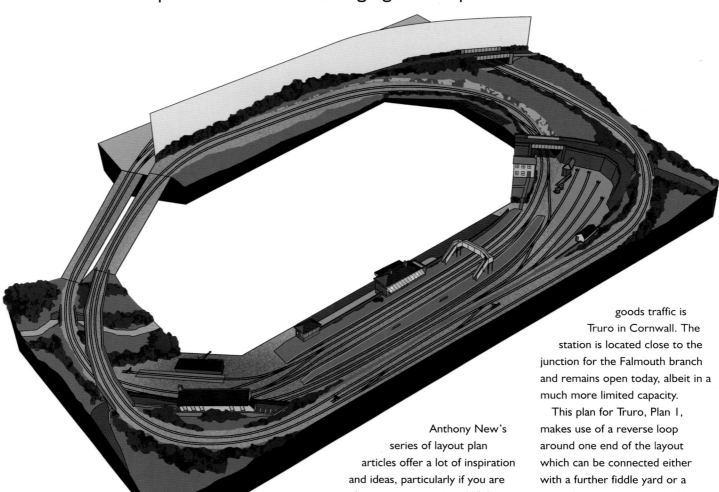

What do you do when you've got a blank canvas for a model railway? You might already have built your baseboards or set aside a dedicated room. It could be large, it could be small, but whichever it is, there is always a solution to fitting in a model railway.

Anthony New's series of layout plan articles offer a lot of inspiration and ideas, particularly if you are planning a new project. While everyone has different ideas and tastes when it comes to building a layout, we all have one 'want' in common – the desire to 'play' trains.

One of the beauties of today's ready-to-run ranges is the large number of express engines which are available, not least for the former Great Western Railway routes from London Paddington to the west. One station which saw both express, stopping and local passenger as well as a mixture of

goods traffic is Truro in Cornwall. The station is located close to the junction for the Falmouth branch and remains open today, albeit in a much more limited capacity.

This plan for Truro, Plan 1, makes use of a reverse loop around one end of the layout which can be connected either with a further fiddle yard or a second scenic area at point X, perhaps based on the coastal section at Dawlish with a second reverse loop and further storage roads hidden behind the cliff face.

This plans started out as a station scene, but after pondering how to make the tunnel entry look realistic, Anthony remembered Truro and the plan grew a good-sized locomotive shed, platforms and even a couple of carriage sidings behind. Although the sidings are compressed quite heavily the scene should be

Plan 1 - Truro Station
Each square represents 1 foot.

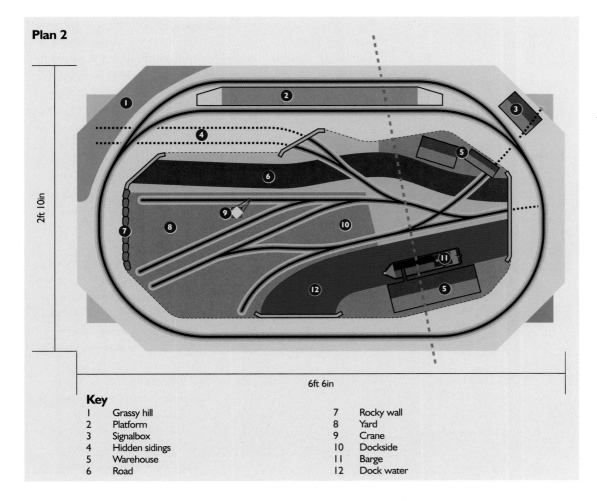

Storage loops behind backscene

Key

1	Semi-detached houses	4	Coal drop	8	Footbridges
2	Turntable	5	Signal Box	9	Station building
3	Engine Sheds	6	Ash	10	Cliff backscene
		7	Water towers	11	Platforms

capable of standing scrutiny as Truro and there are plenty of photographs available in books to work from if you choose to model this wonderful GWR station yourself. Popular views of the shed area show the sheer cliffs behind – an excellent cover for the reverse loop to disappear behind.

There is just about room for a Churchward-style coal stage too, which is seldom modelled properly. The plan is shown as 11ft long, which suits a room of 11ft x 8ft.

Multi-level layouts

We aren't all blessed with a large room to build a layout – some of us have to squeeze our projects in around family life. However, it doesn't mean we have to resort to a straightforward small flat baseboard.

One of the greatest limitations of a small flat baseboard, is that it looks like a small flat baseboard. The simplest way to solve this is not to make it flat! In Plan 2 the layout design makes the most of a split level situation with a 'main' running line positioned on a high level raised section around the outer edges of the baseboard. In order to use second radius curves to accommodate the latest ready-to-run locomotives, the high-level track is out-rigged as shown in the sketch. As the layout is still only

Plan 2

2ft 10in

6ft 6in

Key

1	Grassy hill	7	Rocky wall
2	Platform	8	Yard
3	Signalbox	9	Crane
4	Hidden sidings	10	Dockside
5	Warehouse	11	Barge
6	Road	12	Dock water

33in wide at the corners it is just about practical to store under a bed.

Using set track curved points it is just possible to make a platform loop which will accommodate a second train, and if the layout was set in current times the station could easily be on a singled main line somewhere with one, two, or four-car DMUs on it, or you could run a short HST set, something that has happened from time-to-time. The sketch shows how the whole thing can be constructed.

To add operating interest a dockside has been included inside the layout. There are hidden sidings under the high-level station which act as the rest of the world and it is quite realistic to separate the passenger and freight activities this way as they would, in reality, be combined somewhere more distant and off-stage. A variety of tall warehouses hide the high-level tracks and add visual interest.

Double track in 'N'

When you have only a limited space horizontally you can get more freedom in the third dimension (upwards) as well, and if you use it well it can be extremely effective at disguising the small size of a baseboard.

Plan 3 shows just how much main-line activity can be packed into a small space in 'N' gauge – track and trains that are half the size of 'OO'. The layout is heavily biased towards passenger operation and is designed for the operator who loves to collect main-line locomotives and coaches. The track plan is in fact a fairly basic double-track out-and-back layout in which the reverse loop (which represents the rest of the world) has been placed in the centre of the baseboard and turned into a busy city station to make the most of all the trains that will be stored there.

The low-level station will hold at least four long trains and several DMUs, and the high-level station will hold another two or three as well, though more could be added with a few more inches on each side. The low-level station is designed to be very simple to operate – in fact it is really just a way of disguising the storage of several trains without actually hiding them from view, and the high-level terminus is intended to provide the majority of the operating interest. There is room for a good-sized locomotive shed near the terminus which should house the rest of the locomotive stud, and this can easily be modified to suit steam or diesel periods.

It would not be difficult to add a low-level junction to give a continuous run, but I have deliberately avoided this to force realistic operation and show how even a small layout can be operated prototypically without need for a dedicated fiddle-yard. Construction is straightforward, though I have suggested a removable board on the right-hand edge of the baseboard which houses a complete town scene and can be lifted off for access to the tracks underneath.

If I was building this layout I would probably set it around 1961 so I could run steam engines and green diesels, but it could easily be set in more recent times with HSTs and steam train charters. Of course in a layout designed primarily for operation like this one, you don't actually have to pick a date at all – you can run whatever you feel like on the day. But if you want the greatest realism you have to appreciate that a lots of things changed over forty years, including cars, road signs, and building techniques.

Bristol basis

A station doesn't just have to be part of the scenic area, it can also be turned into a storage area allowing a layout to be wrapped around four sides of a room, making the most of the available space.

Plan 4 is inspired by Bristol Temple Meads, but is by no means an absolute replica of this tremendous, and imposing, station. The track plan uses scenic elements from the site including

Plan 3

Each square represents 1 square foot. Not to scale

Key

1	Factory	6	Terraced houses
2	Turntable	7	Road
3	Coal Staithes	8	Low-level platforms
4	Engine shed	9	High-level platforms
5	Oil tanks	10	Station Buildings
		11	Removable town scene over running lines

Bath Road girder bridge and the idea of a large overall trainshed roof with the platforms curved at one end – although Bristol's platforms are curved virtually throughout their length. These components have been arranged differently in the plan to give it a feeling of familiarity, but also novelty.

Many people, I suspect, would automatically put a large station on the longest baseboard but this has been avoided to allow a long main line to run along the full length of the 'back' wall instead. As for operation, trains can terminate in the through platforms to avoid the need for reverse loops and, as this forces a change of locomotive, it a realistic movement.

The locomotive shed in is intended to be added at a later date as the layout grows, and I think it is very important on a home layout to allow room for it to grow like this. The shed can hold a lot of locomotives and being an inch or so higher than the main line the new baseboard can be simply screwed on top of the old one with a slope for locomotive access. If you choose to build this layout with diesel locomotives, rather than steam, the turntable could be replaced with a 'new' shed and oil-storage tanks or maybe a washing plant.

Goods facilities are limited so the layout as drawn will suit fans of passenger trains best, though there is scope for parcel trains in both directions if the far terminal road is kept for parcels and arriving trains are reversed into it. But you could also model Pyle Hill goods depot (or indeed some private industry) in the space between Bath Road and the locomotive depot if you want.

Double circuits
When planning a layout one of the key things to consider is what your layout is for. Some modellers like to operate a station and don't care if the trains immediately disappear into a tunnel or fiddle yard. Some love to create a single beautiful railway scene through which a succession of trains pass from some hidden storage loops.

If you like to know where the train goes, then Plan 5 could be for you. It doubles the length of the continuous run by allowing trains to run twice around the room before finishing their journey.

The folded figure-of-eight is a very flexible layout idea and in this plan it is inspired by the steeply graded, and well-known, Lickey Incline. The station is based on Bromsgrove and although it has been altered heavily to fit the space available it still provides facilities for banking – where extra locomotives were attached to the rear of heavy trains to assist on the steep gradient - which are usable on the model.

If you are building this layout note that only the goods sidings are flat, though they weren't on the prototype! Everything else is on a gradient: 1-in-100 through

Plan 4
Each square represents 1 square foot. Not to scale

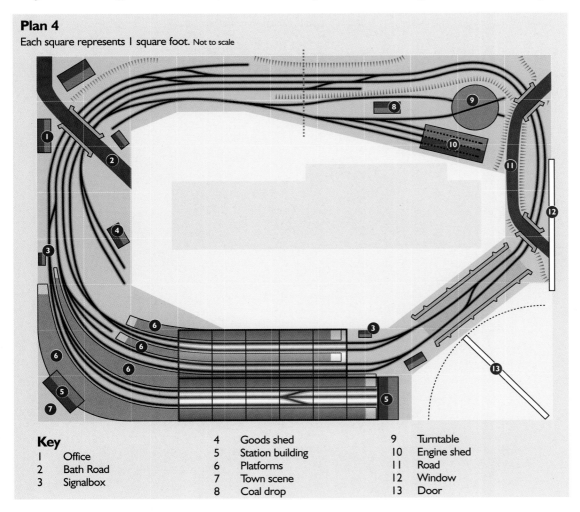

Key
1	Office	4	Goods shed	9	Turntable
2	Bath Road	5	Station building	10	Engine shed
3	Signalbox	6	Platforms	11	Road
		7	Town scene	12	Window
		8	Coal drop	13	Door

the station and storage loops, 1-in-48 elsewhere. The real Lickey bank rose at a gradient of 1-in-37, but I wouldn't recommend copying this unless you are prepared to bank almost every train – this gradient being simply too steep for standard out-of-the-box locomotives, at least with a descent length train. A backscene is used to hide the storage loops, but they could be covered by a removable scenic baseboard if preferred.

In LMS and BR days pairs of 'Jinty' 0-6-0Ts provided most of the banking though various other locomotives were also tried including ex-GWR pannier tanks, BR '9F' 2-10-0s and the unique 'Decapod' 0-10-0 58100 'Big Bertha' which was built specifically for the Lickey Incline. Banking engines used to wait in the central

loops at top and bottom of the incline, but in latter days the one at Bromsgrove was used as a down fast line and the siding at the other end of the station was used for bankers. Useful information including track plans and photographs of the real stations at Bromsgrove and Blackwell can be found in *An Historical Survey of Selected LMS Stations Vol.2* by Preston and Powell Hendry.

Modelling the real railway
Plan 6 is designed to capture a real railway location in its entirety with little compromise. It could easily occupy at least two operators at any one time with the main lines and goods operated independently. Plan 6 is based on the usual practice of choosing a section of a railway route and

turning it into model. The famous Somerset and Dorset Railway from Bath Green Park to Evercreech Junction and Bournemouth has always held great fascination for modellers, not least because of the varied locomotives and rolling stock which traversed this truly cross country route.

The plan is based around the section between Shepton Mallet and Masbury tunnels. As the viaducts of the S&D are so memorable, it is nice to be able to include two of them – Bath Road and Charlton viaducts. To do this Shepton Mallet station has been shortened to fit within an 11ft x 8ft room, although you might prefer to miss out one of the viaducts and extend the station to nearer its true length.

However, the curvature of the line fits the room quite well with

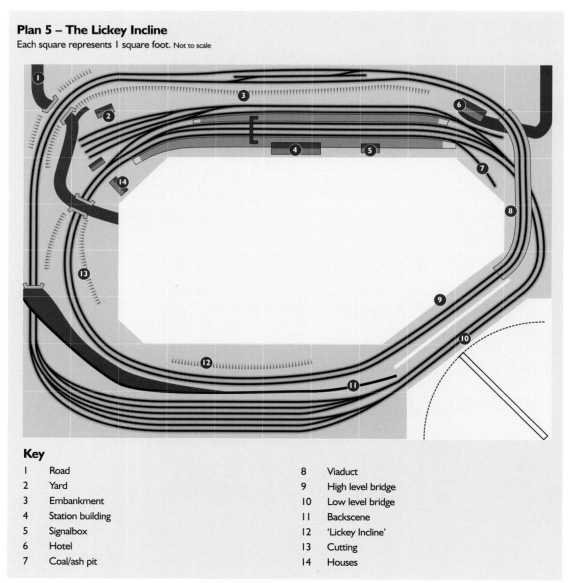

Plan 5 – The Lickey Incline
Each square represents 1 square foot. Not to scale

Key

1	Road		8	Viaduct
2	Yard		9	High level bridge
3	Embankment		10	Low level bridge
4	Station building		11	Backscene
5	Signalbox		12	'Lickey Incline'
6	Hotel		13	Cutting
7	Coal/ash pit		14	Houses

Plan 6 - Shepton Mallet

Each square represents 1 square foot. Not to scale

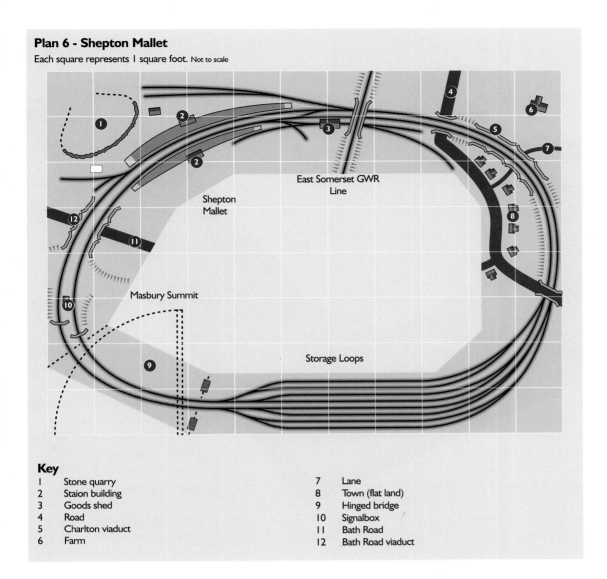

East Somerset GWR Line

Shepton Mallet

Masbury Summit

Storage Loops

Key

1	Stone quarry	7	Lane
2	Staion building	8	Town (flat land)
3	Goods shed	9	Hinged bridge
4	Road	10	Signalbox
5	Charlton viaduct	11	Bath Road
6	Farm	12	Bath Road viaduct

only a little exaggeration and the result is quite pleasing to the eye. The plan could be expanded and straightened a little to suit a club layout and would certainly keep several people busy building it.

Masterpiece

Leeds offers a wonderful complexity of railway lines which grew out of the 19th century railway boom. The area around Leeds had stations built by the Great Eastern, North Eastern, Lancashire & Yorkshire (LYR), London & North-Western (LNWR), and Midland Railways as well as goods depots (some of them jointly).

The centrepiece of this was arguably Leeds Central which disappeared at the end of steam, although it did see English Electric 'Deltics' in regular service just before closure. Fortunately the prototype itself was extremely cramped, due to its city centre location, and would no doubt have been rebuilt after the war if plans had not been afoot to rebuild the 'new' station to the South.

Many long-distance passenger trains, including a few named ones such as the 'Yorkshire Pullman', visited Leeds en route, reversing direction with a new locomotive on the other end, so the layout design allows this to be modelled. Don't forget there were many local passenger trains for every long-distance express and local passenger trains can be run via Holbeck High Level station on the Bradford and Huddersfield line, and via Gerrard Junction on the lines to Harrogate and York.

However, with a little compression, and accepting that compromises will have to be made, Leeds Central can be fitted into an

11ft x 8ft room and Plan 7 is the result.

In this space there is insufficient room for the gradients of the prototype, and the main lines form a simple out-and-back run through a single set of storage loops. Although this has some drawbacks it does allow a decent scenic run and is much easier to operate single-handed. The station is hardly changed, except for compression, but the high and low-level goods depots have been merged; Northbound goods trains can arrive in the station and be shunted down to the low-level goods depot.

Of course one difference between a garage space and a normal room is the position of the door. In Plan 7 I have suggested that the reverse loop hinges up to the end wall, the opposite to the usual arrangement. If this is non-scenic it can fold flat to the wall and

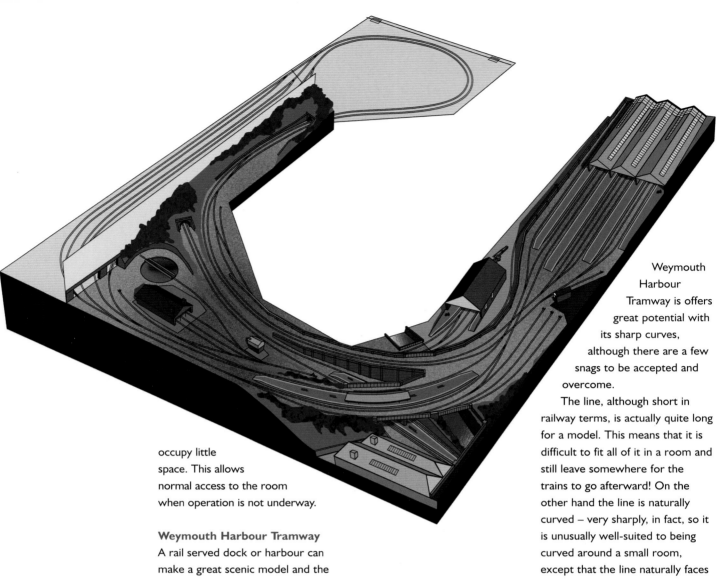

occupy little
space. This allows
normal access to the room
when operation is not underway.

Weymouth Harbour Tramway
A rail served dock or harbour can
make a great scenic model and the

Weymouth
Harbour
Tramway is offers
great potential with
its sharp curves,
although there are a few
snags to be accepted and
overcome.

The line, although short in
railway terms, is actually quite long
for a model. This means that it is
difficult to fit all of it in a room and
still leave somewhere for the
trains to go afterward! On the
other hand the line is naturally
curved – very sharply, in fact, so it
is unusually well-suited to being
curved around a small room,
except that the line naturally faces

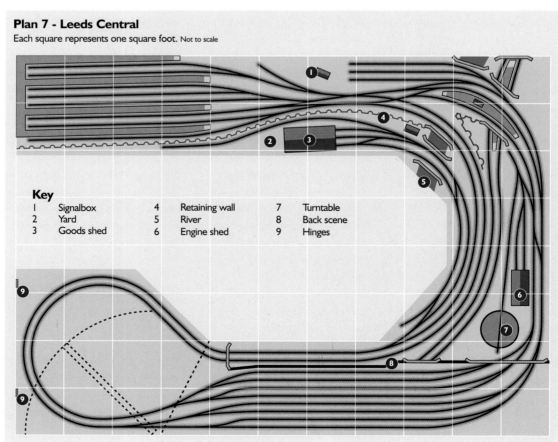

Plan 7 - Leeds Central
Each square represents one square foot. Not to scale

Key

1	Signalbox	4	Retaining wall	7	Turntable
2	Yard	5	River	8	Back scene
3	Goods shed	6	Engine shed	9	Hinges

outward rather than inward, so if it goes around the walls you don't get as good a view as you would hope for.

It is one thing to model Weymouth's harbour tramway, but it is more difficult to model the complete setting including the main line station, and this will add greater operational interest to a layout based on this prototype. For most of its life until Bo-Bo diesels came along in the 1960s, the extreme curvature of the harbour tramway line meant it never permitted express engines on its metals – they were all taken off at the town station and replaced by shunting locomotives such as short-wheelbase ex-GWR '1366' 0-6-0PTs. Due to the sharp curves the coaches were even uncoupled and special longer couplings added between vehicle, though this won't be a problem for our models!

But this does mean that after all the effort of building a layout you can never operate any of your main line locomotives on your layout which is not ideal if (like me) you have accumulated a lot of them! If you want to run these as well then you will need to model the town station, and Plan 8 shows one way of doing this. Here the room needs to be 9ft x 12ft.

Weymouth town station, at its peak, was a very large station and the track plan has been compressed heavily to fit in a 9ft x 12ft room. The result is little cramped, but it could be opened out if a garage size room, say 16ft x 8ft, was available. As the station was the effective terminus for many long-distance trains it is worthwhile modelling even in the space shown – photographs show both *Flying Scotsman* and *Sir Nigel Gresley* there in the 1960s in addition to the usual ex-SR 'Pacific' and GWR 4-6-0 express locomotives which were the daily bread and butter of passenger

operation. Of course, BR diesels would have run there as well, the BRCW Type 3 (later Class 33) being a prime example.

A short spur to a hidden siding represents the Portland branch and would be run with a DMU or auto-coach. Some of the sidings at the station have been included, but those familiar with the station will note the locomotive depot is missing. This is not simply due to a lack of space, but because of the way the fiddle yard needs to operate. A main line train which leaves the station enters the fiddle yard, and the locomotive runs to an isolating section at the end of the siding and stops, preferably over a long uncoupling ramp. But how do we get a new engine on the other end without hand-shunting?

Simple. A locomotive that has previously arrived at the station departs for the locomotive depot which is also off-scene, and in

Plan 8 - Weymouth Harbour Tramway
Each square represents one square foot. Not to scale

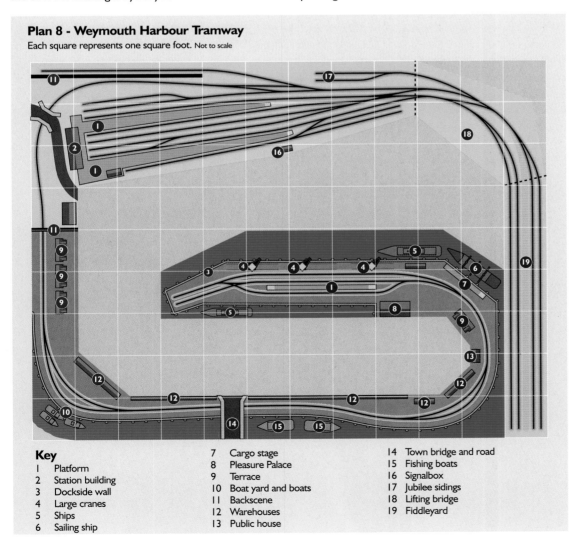

Key

1	Platform	7	Cargo stage	14	Town bridge and road
2	Station building	8	Pleasure Palace	15	Fishing boats
3	Dockside wall	9	Terrace	16	Signalbox
4	Large cranes	10	Boat yard and boats	17	Jubilee sidings
5	Ships	11	Backscene	18	Lifting bridge
6	Sailing ship	12	Warehouses	19	Fiddleyard
		13	Public house		

reality backs onto the train waiting in the fiddle yard. Some later time, when the train has left the fiddle yard and arrived at the station, the locomotive can be released from the isolating section. It leaves the unseen depot and backs out to the station. So you can see that adding a proper engine shed and turntable at the station makes this sleight-of-hand impossible unless another turntable is put on the fiddle yard, which needs more space again and somebody to operate it.

By the seaside

For many of us our first and most nostalgic memories of railway travel were on day-excursions to the seaside or journeys for an annual summer holiday in the South-West of England.

After the Second World War it took a few years for rationing to end and prosperity to begin, but by the 1950s almost everybody fancied following the invitation of the poster-painters to head south — because, as the Southern Railway so memorably put it, "summer comes earlier in the south."

Idyllic paintings of St. Ives, Penzance, and Padstow drew our families to the seaside and the train

journeys, as private cars were still scarce before 1960, made the journey all the more thrilling. So what more natural choice is there for a railway modeller than a seaside station?

The seaside station has a lot of practical benefits for the modeller — many of them were compact termini so they don't have to take up too much space, and yet received a wide range of main line locomotives too.

A favourite location in the South West was Kingswear, in South Devon. This was one of the few main line termini to be single-track and yet it not only saw express steam locomotives in the 1950s, but still does today thanks to its use as a preserved railway and its continued connection to the national network at Paignton.

Plan 9 shows how Kingswear might be turned into a layout in a moderately large room, although it will need a fiddle yard adding beyond the tunnel to accept and dispatch trains. The track plan is as accurate as possible for the period from about 1930, when the re-modelling and extending of the platform was finished, to 1967 when the carriage sidings were removed.

Although compressed a little in length, the station is close to scale in width and the platforms will hold six or seven-coach trains. In a smaller space I would paint the roadway on the backscene and either bend the boathouse sidings around the corner or use the boathouse to hide the entry to the storage sidings. I have shown the footpath to the pontoon for the passenger ferry, but not the slipway to the car ferry the other side of the hotel; this would take another foot or so to model fully.

The carriage sidings are unusual in that they hold only about three coaches each, so a train has to be split in half to store it, although this does add to the operational interest, and the length of headshunt in the bay platform limits this as much as the siding length. The short loop on the bay platform line is not intended as a run-round point, but to allow access to the turntable when the bay platform is full. As you will appreciate, passenger trains tend to arrive at a seaside station in groups and the stock needs to be kept somewhere until they need to leave again. Stock would fill the sidings on summer Saturdays and some would be sent back to Paignton and beyond.

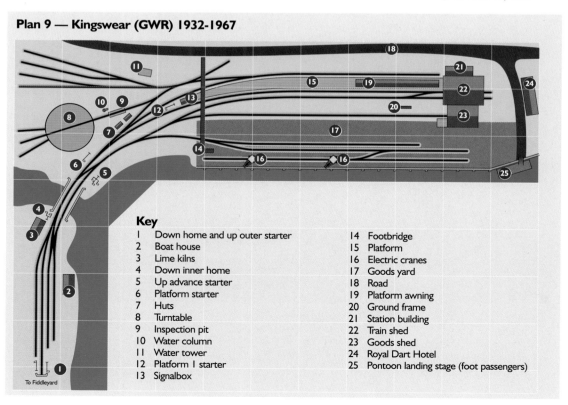

Plan 9 — Kingswear (GWR) 1932-1967

Key

1	Down home and up outer starter	14	Footbridge
2	Boat house	15	Platform
3	Lime kilns	16	Electric cranes
4	Down inner home	17	Goods yard
5	Up advance starter	18	Road
6	Platform starter	19	Platform awning
7	Huts	20	Ground frame
8	Turntable	21	Station building
9	Inspection pit	22	Train shed
10	Water column	23	Goods shed
11	Water tower	24	Royal Dart Hotel
12	Platform 1 starter	25	Pontoon landing stage (foot passengers)
13	Signalbox		

To Fiddleyard

One of the particular attractions of Kingswear was that, like Weymouth, it dealt with a lot of non-passenger traffic too. For many years it was a main coal import dock, serving Torquay Gasworks amongst other businesses, and had cranes there for the purpose, though these are gone today.

I have deliberately telescoped the main line to use the tunnel as a scenic break for the fiddle yard, but the plan could be extended around the room to model either more of the main line, or perhaps the next station at Churston. This is probably a good point to remind you that Kingswear, like other lines that are still open today, can be viewed on-line on Google Maps. Alternatively you could visit the location today, as the Paignton and Dartmouth Railway – *www.paignton-steamrailway.co.uk* – still operates the route from Paignton to Kingswear with preserved steam for tourists and holiday makers.

North of the border
Scotland is very much a land of contrasts and it's always fascinating to leave the city bustle of Glasgow, Edinburgh, or Inverness and cross the rugged Highlands with their stark glacial valleys and dominating mountains to reach the gentler lochs and isles.

The West Highland Extension from Fort William to Mallaig offers great scenic potential to the modeller. The station is still extant today, although a shadow of its former glory in LNER and BR steam days when tourist traffic kept the little fishing town alive and bustling.

Plan 10 is based on the water side terminus of Mallaig. The line was built with a government grant for the benefit of the fishing industry, but its fame as a tourist line prompted the LNER to run through sleeper trains from London King's Cross briefly, though they later terminated at Fort William, as indeed they still do today, although they now run from London Euston up the West Coast Main Line. The LNER also operated rail cruises in the 1930s and observation cars operated there into BR days.

From nationalisation BR operated the route with a mixture of ex-LNER and ex-LMS classes including ex-LNER 'K1' and 'K4' 2-6-0s. The BR 'Standard Four' 2-6-0s also made appearances, most memorably 76001 which was the first of the class to reach Mallaig.

Class 27 diesels were a mainstay of the line in the BR era after the demise of steam, but today the line once again features steam travel in summer months, and the line even appeared in a Harry Potter film, an achievement it shares with the North Yorkshire Moors Railway.

One of the interesting differences between Highland termini and the Southern resorts like Kingswear is the proportion of passenger to goods traffic. Even on the road to the isles there was simply never enough passenger traffic to match the intensive holiday excursions of South West England. However, in the wild open Scottish highlands where the long, twisty and narrow roads deterred motorised competition right up to the 1970s, there was plenty of freight, both general goods and fish.

As drawn the plan for Mallaig fits into a space roughly 7ft x 11ft, but would look good as an island in a much larger space where visitors could see it better and where the operator could walk around it. I have shown the baseboard significantly bigger than needed because the sea and rocks around the line are part of the atmosphere.

Plan 10 — Mallaig

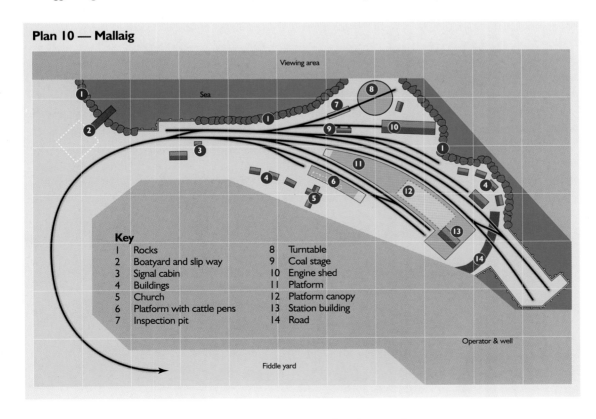

Viewing area

Sea

Key

1	Rocks	8	Turntable
2	Boatyard and slip way	9	Coal stage
3	Signal cabin	10	Engine shed
4	Buildings	11	Platform
5	Church	12	Platform canopy
6	Platform with cattle pens	13	Station building
7	Inspection pit	14	Road

Operator & well

Fiddle yard

Bachmann's 'OO' Class 108 DMU.

Review of the year: 2007-2008

Since the beginning of 2007 there have been countless exciting new announcements and releases. MIKE WILD relives the 18-months from January 2007-August 2008 and highlights the best ready-to-run models in a great period for railway modellers. *Photography, Mike Wild.*

There has never been a time when the model railway hobby has been so diverse and exciting. New announcements are coming thick and fast, and the range of ready-to-run models is increasing all the time as manufacturers bring modellers more of what they want.

'OO' gauge remains as the most popular scale, and it shows. In March 2007 ViTrains, an Italian model company, began distributing its new Class 37/4 model through the Hobby Company of Milton

Keynes, while the big players, Bachmann, Heljan and Hornby, continued to expand their ranges of locomotives, carriages and wagons throughout the year and into 2008.

In a move that caught many by surprise, Dapol Model Railways announced its return to the 'OO' gauge ready-to-run market in 2009 with its first new locomotive model in this scale: a North British Locomotives Class 22 hydraulic. With five major players, plus the ever-busy kit manufacturers, there has never been a better time to

start a new layout.

During 2007 and the first half of 2008 the ready-to-run manufacturers released more than 20 new locomotives from 'N' to 'G' scale and there are many more in the pipeline. At the end of August, Bachmann's new BR 'Standard Four' 4-6-0 was just weeks away and the company was also working on an LMS Fowler parallel boiler 'Patriot' 4-6-0, a Cravens Class 105 DMU, and a Network Rail multi-purpose vehicle. Meanwhile Hornby was developing a new SR

Hornby's Maunsell 'King Arthur' 4-6-0.

ViTrain's Class 37/4.

'Schools' 4-4-0, a BR 'Standard Four' 4-6-0, a Class 153 single railcar and all-new HST power cars as well as the eagerly awaited SR Drummond 'T9' 4-4-0 which was expected to hit the shops in September 2008.

Danish manufacturer Heljan had committed to the production of a limited edition model of Brush prototype *Kestrel* Co-Co, following its sell-out success with a limited edition model of 1961 Brush prototype *Falcon* at beginning of 2008. Heljan has also committed to a model of the British Thompson Houston Class 15 Bo-Bo and a Clayton Class 17 Bo-Bo – and that's just in 'OO' gauge.

Elsewhere, there have been other bold announcements. Kernow Model Rail Centre has commissioned Dapol to produce a ready-to-run model of the North British Class 41 D600 'Warship' and, to the surprise of many, a ready-to-run Southern Region Class 205 Diesel Electric Multiple Unit. Model railway retailing giant Hattons of Liverpool has commissioned Heljan to produce a ready-to-run 'OO' model of the Swindon-built Class 14 0-6-0 diesel hydraulic too, making this an exciting time for diesel followers

In 'N' gauge, Bachmann, which now owns the Graham Farish range, and Dapol have been busy developing new products, with a Class 42/43 (D800 series) 'Warship' arriving in August to be followed by a new Brush Class 47, English Electric Class 08, a Class 108 DMU and a rebuilt Fowler 'Royal Scot'

4-6-0 from Bachmann, and a Class 67, Class 156 and 'B17' 4-6-0 all in the offing from Dapol.

January 2007

The beginning of each year is traditionally a time of new announcements, and January 2007 was no exception! Hornby announced its new projects on January 1 and amongst the highlights was the promise of a Maunsell 'King Arthur' 4-6-0, an Ivatt rebuilt 'Patriot' 4-6-0, a Stanier rebuilt 'Royal Scot' 4-6-0 and a Stanier '4MT' 2-6-4T for steam modellers, plus a new BR Class 56 diesel locomotive and a new range of Southern Railway Maunsell carriages. The new announcements also took in new Skaledale buildings including a locomotive coal drop,

retaining walls, a range of gas works buildings, and more.

The start of the year also marked the arrival of Bachmann's all-new Class 108 DMU. This became the first new first generation Diesel Multiple Unit (DMU) to be turned into a ready-to-run model since Lima had introduced its Class 101 in the 1990s. The 108, however, marked a step-change in quality.

Rather than being a representation of the prototype, this model achieved a level of detail which had been unheard of for a DMU model in 'OO', with properly proportioned underframe detail, a superbly-made body shell and interior lighting. For good measure, the new standard Digital Command Control 8-pin decoder socket was included in the units.

Below: OO Works Drummond '700' 0-6-0.

Bottom: Bachmann's 'N' gauge Class 57.

The 108 was something of a revelation, not least because finally Bachmann was offering a DMU with the standard of detail which is now expected of ready-to-run locomotives.

At the end of the month the London Toyfair took place where Bachmann announced new models for both its Branchline 'OO' range and Graham Farish 'N' gauge ranges.

Newly announced in 'OO' was a model of the ex-LNWR 'Super D' 0-8-0, filling a niche in the freight locomotive market, as well as committing to production of a new range of BR standard 10ft wheelbase box vans including planked and plywood sided versions and insulated vans. A new model of the 29-tonne VDA van and BDA bolster wagon were also announced for modern railway modellers.

In 'N' gauge, Bachmann revealed its intention to produce a model of the BR '9F' 2-10-0 and Ivatt '2MT' 2-6-0 as well as completely re-tooled versions of the BR Class 37 with original split-headcode and centre-headcode designs. Other new releases expected during the year and on show included the all-new 'Jubilee' 4-6-0 and 'Warship' B-B hydraulic.

February 2007

The first of the re-issues of the ex-Lima Class 101 DMU were released by Hornby during February. This wasn't a completely new model, as it relied extensively on the ex-Lima tooling, but they featured a re-worked motor and a Digital Command Control (DCC) socket as standard.

Around the same time, the first versions of the ex-Lima Class 121 arrived from Hornby and Base Toys also began distributing its new range of 'OO' scale budget road vehicles with a range of different cab styles and bodywork.

March 2007

On March 9, the first issue of *Hornby Magazine* went on sale. Around the same time, ViTrains released its first new model – the Class 37/4 diesel.

The new model, which had its roots with Lima, marked a step-change, as it featured a high-performance chassis and a detailed body moulding with removable details, such as the exhaust ports and bonnet front, to allow further variations to be modelled. The first versions to be released were 37428 *David Lloyd George* in BR large logo blue, 37414 in Regional Railways livery, 37403 *Glendarroch* in Railfreight Distribution colours and 37423 *Sir Murray Morrison* in BR Main Line livery.

April 2007

Following its announcement at the start of the year, Hornby released its new model of the Southern Railway 'King Arthur' 4-6-0 express passenger locomotive. The new model featured a stunning level of detail, particularly in the cab, where gauge glasses, pipework, regulator and gauges were all to be found in miniature.

Four versions were released initially: 30453 *King Arthur*, 30764 *Sir Gawain* and 30803 *Sir Harry Le Fise Lake* in BR lined green plus 736 *Excalibur* in Southern Railway olive green.

In 'N' gauge, Bachmann released the first of its brand-new Class 57 models. Compared with previous 'N' gauge releases, save the new Class 66 released in 2006, the 57 offered an unparalleled level of detail for a British outline model in this scale, with a high-performance chassis, working directional lights and a 6-pin decoder connection factory fitted to the chassis. Three versions were released: 57601 in Porterbrook purple, 57301 *Scott Tracy* in Virgin Trains colours, 57003 *Freightliner Evolution* in Freightliner green and yellow and 57602 *Restormel Castle* in First Great Western livery.

During April, Hornby also released its new Elite digital

controller and Skaledale items including retaining walls and a locomotive coal drop.

A new entrant to the 'OO', 1:76 scale, road vehicle market was Oxford Diecast when it released a Morris Minor van and Ford Anglia ice cream van.

May 2007

Following the success of its first batch of Bulleid rebuilt 'West Country'/'Battle of Britain' 4-6-2 and Maunsell 'King Arthur' 4-6-0s, Hornby announced four new versions of each for the autumn. The chosen locomotives were Bulleid 'Pacifics' 34019 *Sir Trafford Leigh Mallory*, 34088 *213 Squadron*, 34026 *Yes Tor* and 34036 *Westward Ho!* plus 'King Arthurs' 746 *Pendragon*, 30799 *Sir Ironside*, 30778 *Sir Pelleas* and 30755 *The Red Knight*. 30755 was subsequently replaced by 30742 *King Uther*.

'OO' Works, a small manufacturer producing limited production runs of hand-built, ready-to-run models, released its new model of the Drummond '700' 0-6-0, offering further choice for Southern Railway and BR Southern Region modellers.

June 2007

June marked the arrival of Bachmann's eagerly awaited Brush Type 4, later Class 47. With 512 examples built between 1962 and 1967, and a career which still continues today, it is no surprise

Bachmann's 'N' gauge Class 04.

that this class has been a popular choice for model manufacturers for many years. Hornby and Lima both produced models, and more recently Heljan introduced a high-detail model, although there were discrepancies over the width of the bogie side-frames compared with the body. The latest version of the

Class 47 in 'OO' gauge came from Bachmann in the form of a completely new model.

This model has proved to be another popular release, with four versions being offered initially – D1500 in original two-tone green, D1764 in two-tone green with full yellow cab fronts, 47035 and

ViTrain's Class 37/0.

Bachmann's Class 47.

Bachmann's Ivatt '2MT' 2-6-0.

Dapol's 'N' gauge 'Q1'.

47148 in BR blue and 47404 in the same livery, but with a digital sound chip.

July 2007

At the end of the month Bachmann held its annual open day at its Barwell headquarters for shop owners and media. The big news was Bachmann's decision to fully re-tool its BR 'Standard Four' 4-6-0 which, when released, would result in a full set of BR 'Standard Fours' from the manufacturer – namely the 2-6-4T, 2-6-0 and 4-6-0. The new tooling is destined to replace the ageing 1970s tooling for the 'Standard Four' 4-6-0.

The latest release from Bachmann arrived in July in the form of the Ivatt '2MT' 2-6-0. This locomotive marked a change from the company's usual practice, as the DCC decoder socket was located in the tender. However,

it was well received and initially it was released as 46521 in BR lined green, 46440 in BR lined black and as 6402 in LMS plain black.

ViTrains increased its range during July too, with release of the first Class 37/0 variants on its increasingly popular bodyshell.

August 2007

During August Hornby announced that it would be re-introducing the ex-Lima six-wheel milk tanker, but with a completely new chassis and NEM coupling pockets. Dapol also announced its intention to produce an 'OO' scale ready-to-run model of the Freightliner and GB Railfreight operated FEA spine wagon for release in 2008.

During the month, Hornby released its first new versions of the ex-Lima Class 66 freight locomotives in three colour schemes – EWS, GB Railfreight and GBRf Medite liveries.

August 2007 was a great month for 'N' gauge modellers with four brand-new releases reaching the shops. First out was Peco's model of the Collett '2251' 0-6-0. Peco hadn't produced a ready-to-run locomotive for many years, but this model was notable as the first DCC fitted 'N' gauge model to be released.

Bachmann's tiny, but highly detailed, model of the BR Class 04 diesel shunter arrived soon after and this showed just how good British 'N' gauge was becoming. It was followed closely by the long-awaited BR Class 60 heavy freight diesel locomotive. As the month closed, Dapol's all new 'N' gauge model of the Bulleid 'Q1' 0-6-0 arrived — another excellent model which wowed modellers upon its release.

September 2007

September was a month for London Midland Region modellers, as Hornby's new rebuilt 'Royal Scot' and rebuilt 'Patriot' 4-6-0 models reached the shops. These two models filled a substantial gap in the market and initially Hornby released three versions of each. The 'Royal Scots' chosen were 46102 *Black Watch*, 46140 *The Kings Royal Rifle Corps* and 46146 *The Rifle Brigade* and the 'Patriots' 45512 *Bunsen*, 45531 *Sir Frederick Harrison* and 45545 *Planet* – all in BR green livery. These new releases were well received, except

for the chimney which has since been revised.

The other big news of September was the launch of Hornby's Railroad range of budget locomotives, carriages, wagons and accessories. This new product line made use of discontinued models including the old version of the Gresley 'A3' 4472 *Flying Scotsman*, the Class 08 shunter and others. All of the models are priced between £3.50, for a single goods wagon, and £50.00 for *Flying Scotsman* and offer a cheaper alternative to the highly-detailed ready-to-run models now being produced by Hornby – the aim being to attract more people into the market by offering good running, but lesser detailed models.

October 2007

The tenth month of the year was a busy one! It started with the release of Bachmann's BR 'Standard Four' 2-6-0 of which four versions were produced with different tenders, depending upon their numbers.

The locomotive identities released initially were 76020, 76053, 76069 and 76079.

Next in line were the first of Hornby's Maunsell carriages. These fantastic models set new standards for carriage detail, surpassing even the recently released Hornby Gresley teak and Stanier Period III stock produced in recent years. Four different vehicle types were released initially: brake composites, corridor thirds, corridor firsts and corridor composites.

Hornby also released the first of its new Class 56 models and again this proved to be well worth the wait. The initial releases were 56013 in BR blue and 56049 in BR Railfreight red stripe followed by EWS liveried 56059 and BR coal sector 56128.

But that wasn't all. The National Railway Museum broke new ground by announcing a ready-to-run limited edition model of the prototype Deltic in partnership with Bachmann. The model certainly

caught the public's imagination and the first batch of 500 special edition models sold out within weeks. However, a further batch of 2,500 standard limited edition models were also produced ensuring that there were plenty available.

In 'N' gauge Dapol made a surprise announcement at its first factory open day when it revealed that it would be releasing a model of the BR '9F' 2-10-0 at the Warley National Model Railway Exhibition at the NEC in December and that future production would include a model of the Beyer, Peacock 'Hymek' Bo-Bo and an LNER 'B17' 4-6-0.

Bachmann's Aristocraft 'G' scale arm also launched its Class 66 diesel model – an impressive and large machine at 2ft 5in long!

November 2007

November was a comparatively quiet month as everyone prepared for the annual Warley National Model Railway Exhibition at the

Heljan's *Falcon*.

Hornby's rebuilt 'Patriot' and 'Royal Scot' 4-6-0s.

Hornby's Railroad Class 08
freight pack.

NEC in Birmingham at the beginning of December.

Just before the end of the month, Dapol's 'Hymek' model touched down following its announcement in October, and Hornby completed its set of Maunsell carriages by releasing the brake composites and corridor thirds.

In the news, Bachmann revealed that it would be producing a range of ready-to-use buildings under its Scenecraft banner including a range of colliery buildings, station buildings and other railway and industry related structures.

December 2007
The month started with the Warley National Model Railway Exhibition on 1/2 December and Bachmann released its wireless Dynamis Digital Command Control controller and Stanier 'Jubilee' 4-6-0 at the beginning of the month.

The 'Jubilee' replaced the ageing ex-Mainline tooling for the same class and Bachmann released

three versions initially — 45611 *Hong Kong* in BR lined green with early crests and riveted tender, 45562 *Alberta* in BR lined green with late crests and a flush-sided tender and 5563 *Australia* in LMS crimson with a Fowler 3,500 gallon tender.

The Warley show also marked the launch of two new model railway companies: 'N' gauge manufacturer Ixion Model Railways and specialist 'O' gauge maker Electrifying Trains – the latter specialising in hand-built ready-to-run EMUs.

Later in the month Hornby released its Stanier '4MT' 2-6-4T. This model filled a gap in the LMS passenger tanks and three versions were released initially: 2546 in LMS black, 42437 in BR lined black with late crests and 42468 in BR black with early crests.

December also witnessed a highlight of the year, as

Heljan's limited edition model of 1961 Brush prototype D0280 *Falcon* arrived. Three liveries were released on this one-off locomotive: original lime green and chestnut brown, BR two-tone green with small yellow warning panels and BR blue with full yellow cab fronts. However, only 2,400 *Falcons* were made, split into 800 in each livery.

In the same month Dapol also released its promised BR '9F' 2-10-0 in 'N' gauge and this became another popular model with several number variations being produced. Other highlights of December were Bachmann's first DCC sound fitted Class 37 and Hornby's Maunsell 'Van C' four-wheel brake van to complement the Maunsell carriages.

January 2008
At start of a new year Hornby

Bachmann's BR 'Standard
Four' 2-6-0.

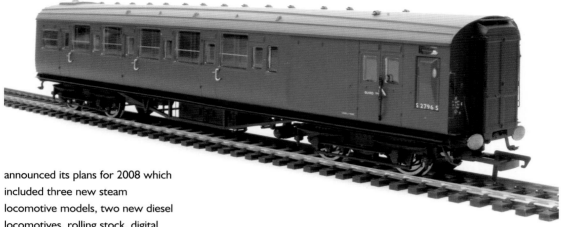

Hornby's Maunsell passenger stock.

announced its plans for 2008 which included three new steam locomotive models, two new diesel locomotives, rolling stock, digital sound fitted models and more.

For steam modellers the highlights were Hornby's announcement of a ready-to-run Drummond 'T9' 4-4-0, the Maunsell 'Schools' 4-4-0 and the BR 'Standard Four' 4-6-0, all of which were expected to be released before the year was out. Hornby also committed to production of much-needed new HST power cars, and a model of the Class 153 single-car DMU. This year, however, the Margate based company opted to concentrate on new goods wagons rather than introduce further new carriages –

the new wagon announcements included a 'Shark' ballast plough and 'Clam', 'Rudd' and 'Tope' engineers' wagons.

Three new ranges were also added to the Hornby catalogue in the January announcement: Skale Scenics, Skale Autos and Skale Lighting, adding further to the range of model railway accessories available through Hornby. Other announcements included new models for Railroad, DCC sound fitted models, a whole host of new buildings for the Skaledale 'OO' and Lyddle End 'N' gauge building range.

During the month Bachmann's new 'N' gauge Class 37 and 'Jubilee' reached the shops, allowing 'N' gauge modellers to purchase two more highly detailed models in this scale, including both split headcode and centre headcode box variations of the 37. The 'Jubilee' boasted impressive new features for an 'N' steam model with its see-through spoked wheels, highly detailed body and, a first for Bachmann at least, a tender-mounted motor. In 'OO' gauge Heljan's Class 58 was released too, offering a much more powerful model of these 1982 introduced Type 5s than Hornby's now obsolete equivalent.

The end of the month saw Bachmann announce further new models at the London Toyfair. At the show, the company revealed that it would be producing an original condition Fowler 'Patriot' 4-6-0, a Cravens Class 105 DMU, a Railtrack Multi-Purpose-Vehicle, a new GWR pattern 8-ton cattle wagon and modern-day Autoballaster wagons in 'OO'

Aristocraft's 'G' scale Class 66, posed with a Bachmann 'OO' gauge Class 66.

gauge. In 'N' gauge, it announced a Class 47 diesel and Class 108 DMU.

February 2008
The much talked about and highly popular National Railway Museum, Bachmann-made model of the prototype Deltic arrived in early February and hit the headlines. It was seen as a bold move, not least because only 3,000 were produced. The model had an extremely high degree of accuracy too, as it was crafted using laser scanning of the 12in to the foot prototype on display at the National Railway Museum's outpost at Shildon.

Hornby was busy too, but rather than locomotives, the company delivered other useful products including the first batch of Skale Autos cars, lorries and buses produced in conjunction with Oxford Diecast. ViTrains also added a new variation to its range in the form of the Class 37/3.

March 2008
March was a month of announcements as Dapol revealed its return to ready-to-run locomotives for 'OO' gauge. The company made public its

decision to produce a model of the North British Locomotive Company Class 22 hydraulic for release in 2009, and shortly after Kernow Model Rail Centre announced a tie-up with Dapol to produce a model of the NBL-built D600 series A1A-A1A 'Warship'.

New start up, Ixion Model Railways also revealed its first model's identity – a GWR 'Manor' 4-6-0 in 'N' gauge.

New releases including Bachmann's superb new 10ft wheelbase 12-ton BR box vans also arrived in the shops, together with

Hornby's Class 56.

Dapol's 'N' gauge 'Hymek'.

Hornby's stunning 'Shark' ballast plough.

April 2008

The fourth month of 2008 prompted several new and exciting announcements from Danish manufacturer Heljan. Following the success of its model of D0280 *Falcon*, the company revealed that it would be producing a 'OO' model of 1968-built Brush prototype HS4000 *Kestrel* for release in 2009.

At the same time, the company also announced that it would produce an 'OO' ready-to-run model of the British Thompson Houston Class 15 Bo-Bo for release in 2009 and a ready-to-run 'O' gauge model of the highly-popular English Electric Class 20. Around the same time, OO Works revealed its next hand-built ready-to-run model would be the Lancashire and Yorkshire Railway Class 23 0-6-0ST.

This part of the year was relatively slow for new releases, although Bachmann bucked the trend by releasing its first Scenecraft buildings and Hornby's Skale Lighting range reached the shops too.

May 2008

New announcements came thick and fast in May with ready-to-run manufacturers announcing no fewer than six new models and the first glimpse of previously announced new items.

Leading the month were the first images of Hornby's HST power cars, Class 153 single railcar and 'Clam', 'Rudd' and 'Tope' engineers wagons. Bachmann pleased 'N' gauge modellers by revealing that it was retooling the Graham Farish Class 08 diesel shunter to offer a fully detailed model with outside frames and it also revealed the first pre-production images of its forthcoming new 'N' gauge Class 47. In Bachmann's Gauge 1 Brassworks range the company announced a ready-to-run 'Black Five' and Class 04 diesel shunter.

Also in 'N' gauge, Dapol announced a new model of the West Coast Main Line Class 86 Bo-Bo 25kV overhead electric locomotive and a complete new range of overhead catenary for 'N'.

Perhaps the most exciting news was Kernow Model Rail Centre's second tie-up with Dapol to produce a ready-to-run model of the Class 205 BR Southern Region Diesel Electric Multiple Unit for release in 2009 – which should fill a massive gap in the market for Southern Region modellers from the transition era onwards.

Hornby bought Corgi for £7.5 million, adding further to the growing portfolio which now includes Airfix, Humbrol, Lima, Jouef, Riverossi and Arnold.

Elsewhere, Hatton's of Liverpool announced its collaboration with Heljan to produce a ready-to-run 'OO' model of the Class 14 0-6-0 diesel hydraulic, and specialist 'O' gauge manufacturer L H Loveless revealed the first pictures of its next

Bachmann's 'OO' gauge Stanier 'Jubilee' 4-6-0.

Hornby's 'Van C'.

Bachmann's
'Super D' 0-8-0.

project – the English Electric prototype Deltic.

New releases included L H Loveless' stunning ready-to-run 'O' gauge 'A4', Bachmann's three-car version of the Class 108 DMU, Oxford Diecast's British Rail maintenance lorries and a range of new Hornby Skaledale buildings.

June 2008
In June, Bachmann released the first images of its pre-production sample of the Fowler parallel boiler 'Patriot' 4-6-0 showing what to expect from this new model. During the same month, the company also launched a new range of trees under the Scene Scapes banner and re-released the 'OO' Class 25 model with directional lights. In 'N' gauge, Bachmann's new standard-setting Stanier 57ft carriages arrived showing, again, just what can be achieved in this scale today.

Dapol announced a brand new 'OO' gauge track cleaner based on the Tomix 'N' gauge 'scrub, vacuum and polish' unit with the aim of release by Christmas 2008 and the first of its new 'OO' gauge goods wagons arrived in the shops: the 9ft wheelbase rectangular tank wagon.

Hornby released new versions of the rebuilt 'Patriot' and 'Royal Scot' 4-6-0s with improved chimneys and NEM coupling pockets at the front and rear and also returned the ex-Lima GWR parcels railcar to the range.

July 2008
The big moment of July was the annual Bachmann open day. At the event Bachmann announced several new models. In 'OO' gauge the company committed to production of a Peppercorn 'A2'

4-6-2 and expansion of the Scenecraft building range with products including a washing plant, a modern servicing depot, a footbridge and more.

The event also provided the first look at Bachmann's long-promised Class 150/1 and 150/2 DMUs, while in 'N' gauge a new model of the Stanier rebuilt 'Royal Scot' 4-6-0 was announced.

Also in the news was Hornby's BR 'Standard Four' 4-6-0 as the first images were released.

July also saw a further batch of Scenecraft buildings reach the shops from Bachmann and the company began distribution of its new range of lorries and cars in conjunction with Base Toys.

August 2008
As the *Hornby Magazine Yearbook* closed for press, Bachmann stepped up and released the eagerly awaited ex-LNWR 'Super D' 0-8-0. Three versions were released initially: 9449 in LMS black, 49395 in BR black with early crests and 49094 in BR black with late crests. Also sneaking in during August was the new 'N' gauge Western Region 'Warship' B-B hydraulic – another wonderful model which shows the potential of 'N'.

On the left is Dapol's 'N' gauge BR '9F' 2-10-0 and on the right is Bachmann's Stanier 'Jubilee' 4-6-0.

In the news, Bachmann revealed that its new BR 'Standard Four' 4-6-0 model, announced in July 2007, was only weeks away from release, and OO Works revealed its next model would be the SECR Wainwright 'H' 0-4-4T.

Looking back over the past 18 months it is easy forget how much has happened, and most it for the better. The range of new announcements is unrivalled with an impressive spread of new models released by all the manufacturers.

Standards have continued to rise and the variety of locomotives, rolling stock, buildings and road vehicles is always increasing. Two of the most prominent releases are the Heljan Brush prototype D0280 *Falcon* and the NRM/Bachmann prototype Deltic. Few, I'm sure, could have imagined that these one off locomotives would ever be available as ready-to-run models, but their popularity must have made them worthwhile investments for the companys behind them.

But the most profound changes have come in ready-to-run 'N' gauge. This was once the ugly duckling of model railways, but with the standard of new products now being produced by Bachmann and Dapol, and particularly the Class 04 diesel shunter and Stanier 'Jubilee' its fair to say we've never had it so good in 'N'.

Who knows what the next 12 months will bring, but, looking back on 2007 and 2008, its bound to offer more exciting and extraordinary models.

The NRM/Bachmann prototype Deltic.

Arrowmouth

The West Coast Main Line of the 1960s offered enthusiasts a great selection of motive power from Stanier's mighty 'Duchess' class 'Pacifics' to BR '9Fs' on heavy freight trains and a range of diesel classes. With scale-length trains, impressive scenery, and a seaside location, the Redditch Model Railway Club's Arrowmouth is a popular fixture on the exhibition circuit. *Photography, Mike Wild.*

B ritish Railway's locomotive fleet was changing rapidly in the early 1960s following publication of the 1955 Modernisation Plan. This document spelt the end for steam traction as it envisaged a new fleet of diesel locomotives and large electrification projects. One such project was the West Coast Main Line from London Euston to Glasgow, but it happened in stages and the section north of Crewe remained in the hands of steam and diesel traction much longer than the London-Crewe section.

It is this area of the country that the Redditch Model Railway Club chose to base this layout on. It is based on the fictional town of Arrowmouth which is located on the north west coast of England close to the real Hest Bank station which once stood between Lancaster and Carnforth.

The railway is still diverse, as this is the 1960s, and steam and diesel traction run side-by-side on everything from crack expresses to

bulk coal trains and mixed goods rumbling their way noisily through the station and over the River Arrow.

Watching the layout, you can almost imagine leaning out of the front carriage window of the 10am 'Royal Scot' from Glasgow Central to London Euston as it bursts out of Arrowmouth tunnel and onto the bridge across the River Arrow hauled by a Class 47 diesel. This is what Arrowmouth is all about, capturing the West Coast Main Line (WCML) as it was in the 1960s during the change over from steam to diesel traction.

Redditch MRC Secretary Guy Craddock commented: "The layout was completed in 1992 and it has been popular on the exhibition circuit from day one. Observers at exhibitions have even said that watching the layout in action is like trainspotting without the wait, and there are even some who believe they have caught a train from this fictitious location!

"Arrowmouth is a continuous run measuring 22ft x 8ft in total and it

includes a station with two through roads, two platform loops and a bay platform together with the distinctive bridge across the aptly-named River Arrow and many other detail features."

The seaside town of Arrowmouth is totally fictional. It follows the Redditch MRC's tradition of naming layouts after places and areas in and around Redditch. The River Arrow actually flows through Redditch, but the layout is based on the north west coast of England far away from the river's true location.

Guy added: "The real West Coast Main Line's proximity to the coast allowed us to model a coastal setting for Arrowmouth – something that was a little unusual back in 1992 – and the era has been set between 1963 and 1968 when steam was in its Indian Summer in this area of the country, and five years before the West Coast Main Line from London to Glasgow was electrified north of Crewe. The station is an ideal place to stop and watch the trains pass by, as Stanier's remaining designs, including '8F' 2-8-0 and 'Black Five'

4-6-0, handle goods trains whilst 'Duchess' and 'Princess' class 'Pacifics' haul the heaviest expresses. Of course that isn't all that appears. Other locomotive designs including the mighty Riddles BR '9F' 2-10-0s, Ivatt '2MT' 2-6-2Ts, '4F' 0-6-0s and Hughes/Fowler 'Crab' 2-6-0s also make appearances at the head of goods and passenger trains alongside the first influx of diesels."

One of the keys to Arrowmouth's package is the range of correctly formed and weathered trains. The group provide their own stock for the club layout, rather than the club owning the stock, and this means that a lot of time and effort has been invested in this part of the project. The locomotives, naturally for a 1960s period exhibition layout, are all weathered and detailed, although the vast majority are ready-to-run with a few kit built examples for good measure. All rail vehicles receive the same treatment when it comes to detailing. Guy commented: "We have had spectators at shows not only taking locomotive numbers, but the numbers of the carriages and wagons running behind them too!"

Rejoining the 10am 'Royal Scot', today hauled by a BR green Class 47, the train enters the scenic section of the layout through Pitcheroak Tunnel

before travelling along an embankment above Park Farm. Soon after the line plunges into Arrowmouth Tunnel to pass through the headland cliffs which protect the properties behind from the ravages of the Irish Sea. It then crosses the bridge over the River Arrow, one of the most prominent features of the layout, before rumbling along the raised sea wall which protects the main town from the sea.

On the approach to the station the train passes under a typical London and North Western Railway

(LNWR) gantry signalbox before crossing the pointwork of the station throat. The 'Royal Scot' passes through non-stop on the centre roads whilst in the platform a '4F' waits patiently with a local train and the station's glass screens rattle as the Class 47 continues its journey south. After the station the line swings inland and passes a farm machinery factory, the mudflats of a small river and campers on the Arrowmouth campsite before disappearing out of view through a deep cutting into the fiddle yard.

[PHOTO] 3 A popular feature of the stock roster is the 'Condor' container train. A pair of English Electric Type 1s (later Class 20) head south through the station.

[PHOTO] 4 The track gang continue their work as Stanier 'Princess Royal' 4-6-2 46203 *Princess Margaret Rose* races through with the daily south bound sleeper train.

📷5 Steam and diesel
locomotives run side-by-
side on Arrowmouth
capturing the changing
face of British Railways.
BR Sulzer Type 2 (later
Class 25) D5211 passes
through the station with
a north bound oil train.

Building Arrowmouth

"Arrowmouth was born out of the
desire to build a new exhibition
layout for Redditch Model Railway
Club's 25th Anniversary in 1992,"
Guy said. "We looked around model
railway shows in the area and
decided to set our new railway on
the coast. The layout was proposed
in late 1990 as a replacement for our
Bordesley Parkway layout, which
had not been seen on the exhibition
circuit for a number of years.

"After many hours of debate
amongst members, the plan for
Arrowmouth was created and it was
an amalgam of a number of ideas put
forward by members of the Club.

The resultant track layout is simple
yet flexible and the continuous run
allows intensive operation of trains
to keep spectators happy at
exhibitions.

"The baseboards are of a
conventional solid top construction
of softwood and chipboard. A sub –
base which carries the track has
been added 2½ in above the solid
top. Again this sub base is made of
chipboard. The result is a very firm
and solid base for the railway, but, as
our members will testify, the boards
are very heavy to carry around. The
whole layout is supported on
trestles, each with a chain to adjust
the height."

Club layouts are often faced with
a decision as to which track type is
best. Some prefer the finer Code 75
version, but some earlier model
locomotives won't run particularly
well on it. Guy commented: "Being a
club layout we decided to use the
universal 4mm scale 'OO' gauge
Code 100 track, as using any of the
finer scales would have meant that
members might have to convert
existing stock to suit the new
layout's particular track type. As a
club, we feel that 'OO' scale track
portrays the railway well enough,
and after all, it is more about
creating the effect of a real railway
that all our members can enjoy."

Virtually all the track has timber
sleepers, although concrete-
sleepered track has been used in the
station area and on one of the
corners. This is typical of the era the
Redditch MRC has modelled, as
concrete sleepered track become
much more widespread during this
period. The track is laid on cork and
then ballasted with loose granite
chippings stuck in place using diluted
PVA glue. Once the track was laid,
the rail sides were painted a rust
colour and the whole formation has

📷6 At the country
end of the layout, a BR
Sulzer Type 4 (later Class
45) bursts out of
Arrowmouth tunnel with
a van train.

since been toned down using a variety of aerosol-spray colours to give it a more 'used' look.

Building the 'townscape'

The Redditch MRC has developed its own method for the construction of buildings. Although it isn't necessarily revolutionary, it does mean that each layout built by the club has totally individual buildings designed to fit the space and the 'real' location of the model.

The basic method revolves around a thick card base structure for each building. This is then covered with either brick papers or plastic card to represent stone or brick finishes. In some cases various grades of sandpaper have also been used to represent concrete rendering, something often found at seaside towns to further protect buildings from the ravages of the sea.

"All the railway buildings are based on London North Western Railway (LNWR) structures and drawings," Guy commented. "The main station building is based on the one that was at St Albans, and the small waiting room and signalbox are based on standard LNWR drawings. In common with many other railway companies, the LNWR produced standard buildings made of wood from panels of a standard size.

Each of these panels would either have a door, window or plain planking or a combination of any of the three. This meant that a building could be formed to fit the purpose and location required by joining these standard panels together.

"We have done just that with the models, as the real railway did, and constructed a waiting room and signalbox by this method. Each building is designed to fit their location and purpose, and is constructed using standard sized panels."

Another key feature of the layout is the pair of glass screens between the platforms and these provoke many questions at exhibitions. Guy takes up the story: "The screens were common on the North Wales Coast route and were used to protect passengers from the

weather and the sea whilst waiting for trains. We constructed ours from scratch using plastic strut 'H' section girder and plastic glazing material to represent the glass. The glazing bars, which were added to the plastic glazing material, were originally made using strips of plastic card painted cream, but we found that it was difficult to stick these strips permanently and they have since been replaced these with thin strips of masking tape which is handily the correct colour!"

The station buildings have been finished by the addition of canopies. These are made from card, as are the valances and they add much to the overall feel of the station. Recent improvements to the layout have included extension of the goods yard and the addition of a loading dock for parcels which

[o]7 An English Electric Type 4 (later Class 40) thunders over the River Arrow. The bridge is entirely scratchbuilt.

[o]8 With a local stopping train behind, Ivatt '2MT' 2-6-2T 41278 potters onto the bridge on the approach to the station.

📷9 ▶ The most prominent feature of the layout is the bridge over the River Arrow. A '4F' 0-6-0, now in its last years of service, passes a Stanier 'Jubilee' 4-6-0, at the head of a train of coal empties.

📷10 ▶ The length of this 22ft long exhibition layout is clear, as a BR Sulzer Type 2 crosses the River Arrow.

involved construction of another new canopy made of card.

The river bridge

The main railway structure, other than the station, is the bridge over the River Arrow. The design is a copy of those found on the Cumbrian coast line, which is close to the area where the layout is based.

"The bridge is constructed around a piece of chipboard as the decking," Guy said. "The stone supporting pillars are made from shaped pieces of wood covered in embossed stone. The track on the bridge has been laid on strips of wood to represent the longitudinal timbers used on the prototype instead of normal sleepers. The railings on each side are made from metal. The uprights are pieces of SMP rail and the railings themselves are pieces of welding rod. These have then been soldered to the uprights and the end result is a very solid and durable structure. In an attempt to get a prototypical noise when trains pass over the bridge, the rails have been notched at scale 60-foot intervals to represent jointed track."

Detailing doesn't stop there though. A pedestrian walkway has been added on the inland side of the bridge, with a sewage pipe on the other.

Operation and presentation

Operation and presentation is something that the Redditch MRC pride themselves on. Guy takes over: "Having a continuous circuit of track on the layout, it is quite obvious that trains leave the fiddle yard and travel round the layout to re-enter the fiddle yard at the other end. This makes the running of the layout very simple and the art is to make what the spectators out at the front as realistic as possible. To make this as interesting as possible, we have a variety of types and lengths of trains. The formation of the track at the front, with the platforms on loop lines off the main line, allows trains to be held in the platforms as non-stop trains race through the centre roads.

"If the layout was started from scratch today then the wiring could have been simplified by the use Digital Command Control (DCC), but at the same time there is some resistance within the club to install DCC chips in their locomotives because of the cost. The layout is wired by the normal common return method, to provide cab control via two control panels. One is situated behind the station whilst the other is next to the tracks in the fiddle yard. All the connections between the baseboards and control panels are made using industrial connectors.

"When the layout is at an exhibition, the club is on show as well. We ensure that all the front boards and the backs of the backscenes are painted black and, more importantly, that they are kept clean. We have mounted spot lamps above the layout to illuminate the railway and hung between two of the lighting uprights there is a railway totem sign. This is a full sized metal replica of a British Railways style station totem made by a specialist manufacturer, which clearly shows the name Arrowmouth to the spectators.

"Arrowmouth has been a popular layout on the exhibition circuit, and we have travelled as far north as Barrow-in-Furness in Cumbria and south to the West of England Model Railway Show in Cornwall with the layout. To date the Arrowmouth has attended 36 shows and traveled over 3,800 miles in the back of hire vans to and from the exhibitions. The layout has been voted best in show on three occasions by the visitors and this means a lot to us, as they are showing their appreciation for the layout.

"As you might expect the Club member's have enjoyed taking Arrowmouth out to display it for the public, and there are more visits to come in the next couple of years – look out for us and say hello!"

Contacting the Redditch MRC

Redditch MRC website: *www.redditch-mrc.com*
General e-mail: *guy@redditch-mrc.com*
Club Secretary and Exhibition Manager: Guy Craddock
Club President: Mick Clements
E-mail: *mick@redditch-mrc.com*
Telephone: 01527 67544

Arrowmouth stats

Owner:	Redditch Model Railway Club
Builder:	Redditch Model Railway Club
Built:	1990-1992
Gauge:	'OO'
Track:	Peco Code 100
Length:	22ft
Width:	8ft
Layout type:	Continuous run
Period:	1960s BR steam to diesel transition

Arrowmouth Track Diagram
(Each square represents 1 square foot: Not to Scale)

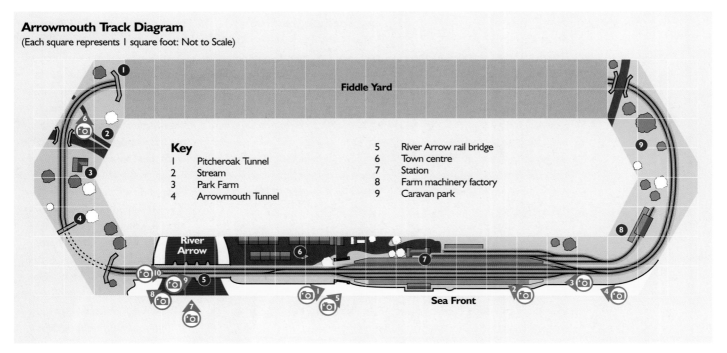

Key
1   Pitcheroak Tunnel
2   Stream
3   Park Farm
4   Arrowmouth Tunnel
5   River Arrow rail bridge
6   Town centre
7   Station
8   Farm machinery factory
9   Caravan park

Fiddle Yard

River Arrow

Sea Front

Baseboards – the ins and outs

A solid baseboard forms the foundation of every model railway. MIKE WILD and IAN MORTON offer tips and techniques for building solid top structures. *Illustrations, John Wiffen.*

No matter how small or large, portable or permanent, every model railway will need some form of baseboard and supporting structure to achieve the best results from model locomotives and trains.

Like buildings, and the real railway, a sturdy foundation will reap rewards in the future for a layout. If it's too flimsy, track might distort and this can lead to unpredictable running or, in the worst case, a layout which becomes unuseable. There are many styles and designs of baseboard. No single design is right for everyone, but the basic methods remain the same.

Most modellers turn to timber for baseboards. By using the right materials a strong and light board can be built and, depending on your circumstances, they can be designed in a modular format so that a large layout can be dismantled when needed or for transport to model railway exhibitions.

Where to start?

Before starting construction, there are some important questions to ask. How big will the layout be? Will it be permanent or portable? How will it be supported? Where will it be based – a spare room, garage or garden shed are the most common locations? And, do you want scenery to rise and fall above the level of the railway?

Size will always be dictated by the space you have available, but the most important decisions are whether it will be portable and if it will have scenery below the level of the railway or just on the same level or above.

A permanent layout could be built simply using 12mm thick chipboard or plywood, but Medium Density Fibreboard (MDF) is less ideal as it is harder to work with due to the fine grain. Plywood combines strength with minimum weight and this makes it ideal for many layouts.

Even for small permanent layouts, a timber framework is preferable as it will avoid any chance of the baseboard top warping or distorting due to changes in room temperature or atmosphere. However, chipboard in particular is a strong manufacturered board that will remain as a flat surface, so long as it has been stored horizontally prior to purchase.

A portable layout needs to be designed in sections that are manageable. Taking Bay Street Shed, *Hornby Magazine* Editor Mike Wild's layout, as an example, the 6ft long scenic area is split into two 3ft x 2ft baseboards. These are connected using coach bolts through the end timbers and, by the use of 6mm thick plywood and 44mm x 18mm timber, the boards are light weight too.

Any number of this style of baseboard can be joined together to form a longer and wider layout so, for example, four 3ft x 2ft baseboards could be bolted together to create a 12ft x 2ft long layout base.

If the layout is only likely to be moved on occasion longer baseboards may be an option, but beyond 4ft long they can be come difficult to handle and there is a greater risk of damage during movements.

Solid top

Solid top baseboards are exactly as they sound. Traditionally they have a timber frame with a solid wooden top of either plywood, MDF or Sundeala, and they are often referred to as 'conventional baseboards'.

This style of baseboard has its limitations as scenery has to be on the same level or above the railway so if you are planning a layout with a viaduct or a railway over road bridge they may not be the best choice. However, by including a dropped baseboard in between two solid top boards a viaduct or rail over road crossing can be introduced.

The main advantages of the solid top baseboard are that they are within the ability of anyone who can saw a piece of timber to length, and they require minimal tools and planning. The solid top also means that the baseboard can be built without knowing exactly where the track or other features will be placed and the size of the layout can be set before track planning starts in some cases. If you want a bit of flexibility, they're a good choice.

Depending on their size and the types of wood used, solid top boards can become heavy to move, but by using light materials, such as 6mm thick plywood and a 44mm x 18mm timber frame, the weight can be kept down, particularly if each board is limited to a maximum of 4ft in length.

Traditionally the timber frame consists of 2in x 1in timber battens (roughly equal to 44mm x 18mm planed timber which is common in DIY stores) forming a grid of 12in to 24in squares. This should be 'prepared' timber which has been planed smooth and dried before purchase, but be aware that the dimensions are nominal for planed timber and there may be differences between individual lengths. If you do come across this situation ensure that the top of the frame is at the same level – the bottom of the frame is less critical and the odd couple of millimetres difference won't cause any problems.

There are different thicknesses of timber to choose from. If you have deep point motors or other large items hidden below the baseboard, or very heavy trains or scenery, then 3in x 1in – roughly 68mm x 18mm – timber may be more suitable.

The choice of wood for the solid top is also important. There are lots of choices in DIY stores – some materials are good, and others are bad when it comes to model railways. Blockboard, chipboard and Medium Density Fibreboard (MDF) are heavy, and blockboard is particularly hard to work. Chipboard is easy to cut, but it won't readily accept track pins and special screws are required because standard screws may cause the chipboard to break at the edges.

As a rule, MDF should be avoided. It won't accept track pins, it is heavy, difficult to work with and

the dust from cutting can be harmful. Insulation board is another option, but this has little strength and is very susceptible to damp and, although it sounds strange, it is too easy to cut which can result in jagged edges.

Plywood is one of the best materials available for solid top baseboards. It comes in a variety of thicknesses and due to the way it is manufactured it is also very strong. It is more expensive than MDF, but, as a rule, you pay for what you get when it comes to plywood. This type of board accepts track pins easily using a pin hammer to tap them home and it is easy to cut with either a hand saw or electric jigsaw and, when less than 5mm thick, it can be cut with a craft knife with ease. In general 6mm plywood will suit most applications, but if you are looking for greater strength 9mm plywood is a safe option. However, thicker plywood can become heavy, which defeats the object of using this lightweight material.

Another alternative is Sundeala board. This is made from recycled newspaper and is easy to cut and drill, accepts track pins easily and also absorbs some of the noise from moving trains. It is supplied in 1200mm x 600mm sheets, but it can be difficult to locate as it is not widely stocked by DIY outlets. The

manufacturer can be contacted directly by calling 01453 540900 or by visiting www.sundeala.co.uk

Joining and aligning

When a layout is split over two or more baseboards they need to be joined and aligned accurately. It is essential that good and consistent alignment is achieved at every join to ensure that trains will cross the joins without derailments and that the scenery doesn't have large gaps

Building a solid top baseboard

Tools – what you'll need

■ Set square
■ G clamps
■ Tenon saw
■ Mitre block
■ Electric jigsaw
■ Screwdriver
■ Electric drill
■ Drill bit set (2mm-20mm is ideal)

Step 1

Cut two lengths of 2in x 1in (44mm x 18mm) timber to the same length as the baseboard top. These will be the two long sides of the frame.

Step 2

Subtract the thickness of two lengths of timber (about 1 ½ in, 36mm) from the width of the baseboard top. Cut five pieces of timber to this length. These will be the short sides of the frame and the cross-members.

If the baseboards are to be permanently fixed in place, each section can simply be screwed together, but if the layout is to be portable then a means of alignment will be required. Coach bolts and split hinges have been used for many years by model railway builders, but more recently cabinet and pattern maker's dowels have come into use to provide more accurate alignment, particularly for smaller scales and finer tolerance gauges such as 'EM' and 'P4'. Wooden dowel rod can also be used in conjunction with coach bolts, but, over time they may wear and loose their accuracy of alignment.

All baseboards, however wide or narrow, will need at least two points of alignment. This could consist of two dowels and one coach bolt, but to avoid any chance of the board joins flexing, two dowels and two coach bolts are preferable. If one coach bolt is used on its own, then the two baseboards will easily twist out of alignment.

Coach bolts were once the primary choice, but regular removal and insertion causes the hole in the baseboards to wear leading, ultimately, to poor alignment. Coach bolts are available in a variety of lengths and diameters and with different heads and various nuts are

available including square, hexagonal and wing nuts. The latter are easier to tighten by hand whereas the other variants will require either a spanner or a socket.

Brass hinges can be used for a simple and quick way to align boards. By fitting the hinge halves either side of a joint, the centre pin can be knocked out using a nail and replaced with a length of metal rod, bent over at the top to stop it falling through the hinge.

Cabinet and pattern makers' dowels provide highly accurate alignment, but coach bolts will also be required, as the dowels offer no means of securing baseboards together.

Step 3

Make sure the timber is firmly held so that it doesn't move whilst cutting it. When using an electric jigsaw, safety goggles are a necessity to avoid getting any sawdust in your eyes.

Step 4

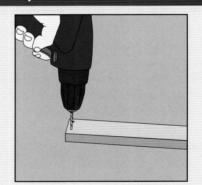

Place one of the long lengths of timber in the workbench. Place one of the short pieces to form an 'L', as shown above. Drill pilot holes for two screws. Apply some wood glue to the join and then screw the two pieces together.

Step 5

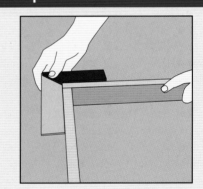

Check that the 'L' is square and adjust if necessary before the glue dries.

Step 6

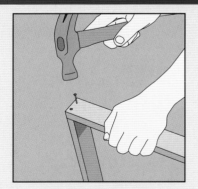

Repeat with the other two identical pieces for the other side and end. You may find it useful to drive the screws in until their points just project from the underside of the side members, line the timbers up and then tap the screws with a mallet to mark their location on the cross member before finally screwing them fully into the holes.

Step 7

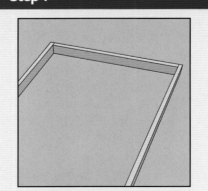

Using the same process join the two 'L' pieces to make a rectangle.

Step 8

Having checked that the frame is square you can now measure the centre beam and cut it to length. To simplify the carpentry work, this is made from 1in x 1in (21mm x 21mm timber.

■ The subject of baseboard construction is expansive and there are many options and designs to consider. The text produced here is based on Ian Allan Publishing's *Aspects of Modelling – Baseboards for Model Railways* by Ian Morton. For a full account of baseboard construction techniques, *Baseboards for Model Railways* can be bought direct from Ian Allan Publishing.

Step 9

The cross-members need to be notched to fit over the centre beam. First measure the centre of the cross-member then use it as the centre line to measure a 21mm wide area for the centre beam to slot into.

Step 10

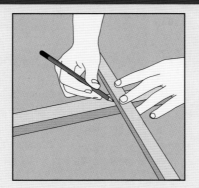

Use a piece of 1in x 1in (21mm x 21mm) timber to mark the width and depth of the slot.

Step 11

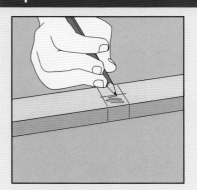

Clearly mark the area that is to be removed to avoid mistakes when cutting out.

Step 12

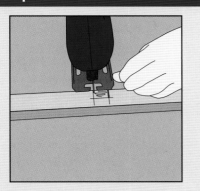

Saw along both sides of the notch. Cut along the inside of the pencil lines.

Step 13

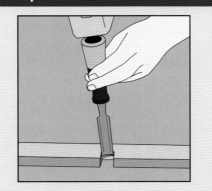

Using a chisel knock out the waste piece. The notch can then be cleaned up, if necessary, with a knife or file. Repeat this process for all cross-members.

Step 14

The centre beam can be screwed and glued in position and then the cross-members can be put in place.

Step 15

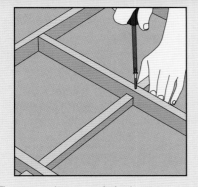

The cross-members are attached with two screws through the side members at each end and one screw into the centre beam.

Step 16

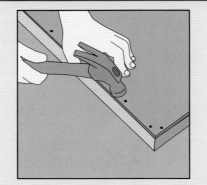

Turn the frame over and nail or screw the baseboard top in place. Nailing or screwing the top to the centre beam and cross-members, as well as the outer frame, will minimise any possibility of bumps and hollows developing.

Step 17

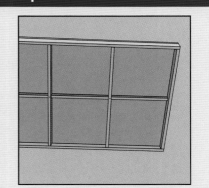

A completed board shown from underneath. You may wish to drill a number of holes in the cross-members for wires to pass through.

Good track work is an essential ingredient of a model railway project after the baseboards. Take care to ensure joins are smooth and correctly aligned.

Tracklaying

MIKE WILD turns the spotlight on tracklaying and shows how set track can be laid using different underlays.

After baseboard construction, track work is the most important part of a model railway. Poorly laid track leads to unpredictable running, derailments and a lack of satisfaction, but good tracklaying means that a layout will run smoothly and offer many hours of entertainment.

There is a bewildering array of track components and underlays available to today's modeller and sometimes it is difficult to decide which is best for your project.

We've concentrated on readily available Bachmann, Hornby and Peco track for this guide. These three ranges are available from virtually any model shop stocking railway equipment and, if you are building a layout with Code 100 track – the standard rail size for 'OO' layouts, the two systems are universal and can be combined together.

The most important thing for good track work is a solid and firm base. This comes in two parts: the baseboards and a suitable track underlay. Like track products,

there are several underlay products available including Peco's foam underlay, Gaugemaster's pre-ballasted underlay, Tracklay's useful self adhesive product and, the simplest of them all, cork.

Your choice depends on what style of finished track you want. If you are likely to change the arrangement, then Peco or Gaugemasters products are a good choice. However, beware, as the Peco foam underlay will deteriorate over time. For the most realistic final result, after ballasting, cork is a good choice. It can be cut to shape to suit any track formation using a craft knife and a steel ruler and is readily available in rolls from model shops or, as an alternative, tiles from DIY shops. Cork allows loose ballast to be applied after tracklaying and glued in place to provide a more realistic finished track and, like all other underlays, it also deadens the sound of passing trains – although less so after ballasting.

Set track is by far the easiest way to construct a first layout, as the sectional pieces of track have pre-drilled holes for track pins and they

UK Track manufacturers

Manufacturer	Products	Website
■ Hornby	Set track, flexi-track, semi-flexible track and points	www.hornby.com
■ Peco	Set track, flexi-track and points	www.peco-uk.com
■ Bachmann	Set track and points	www.bachmann.co.uk

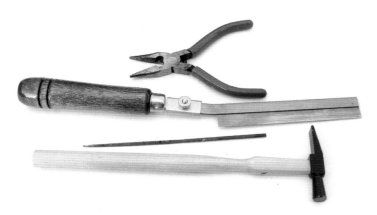

A selection of tools is essential to create the best possible trackwork. From the top: pliers, a hacksaw (or electric mini-drill with a cutting disc), a small file and a pin hammer.

Set track has pre-drilled holes to accept track pins, the latter being available from all model shops. Use a pin hammer to gently tap track pins into the pre-drilled holes to keep the track in place. With this type of underlay, the pins can easily be removed if desired.

come ready fitted with rail joiners at each end, saving another job. Flexi-track requires a little more effort, as rail joiners need to be added to each length, and associated points, and holes will need to be made in the sleepers before track pins are hammered home.

The photographs show offer tips and techniques for making the best of it to ensure that trains run smoothly and that you gain many hours of enjoyment from a new layout.

Tips and techniques

■ A solid baseboard is essential for good track – there is no shortcut to this!
■ Use sectional track to give yourself confidence in tracklaying.
■ Use the Hornby or Peco sectional track 00/HO planbooks as a source of inspiration.
■ Experiment with pieces of track on your baseboard before fixing the track down.
■ Study manufacturers' catalogues to see their full range, and join a club to see how advanced modellers do it.
■ Think to the future – will you want to install point motors to change the direction of a point?
■ Use insulated (plastic) rail joiners combined with a switch to provide a 'section' to park a locomotive.
■ Use the largest radius curves that your baseboard will allow.
■ Do not use 'S' bends unless it is absolutely necessary.
■ Make sure that the rails and fishplates fit together properly. A misaligned fishplate will derail trains. Push the pieces of track together on a flat surface.
■ Be careful when using any type of adhesive near the points. If it seeps into the point changing mechanism you might need to buy a new point!.
■ Use insulated points to reduce the number of electrical connections.
■ Use paper templates available from Peco to see which pieces you need.
■ If you are going to fit point motors – think ahead – where are they going to go?
■ Buy a rerailer for the ease of putting locomotives and rolling stock on the track.
■ Ensure that all your trackwork is accessible for cleaning and derailment purposes.
■ Be relaxed and enjoy the track!

Improving the quality of track

■ The finer the rail the more realistic it will look. So Code 75 track will look more realistic than Code 100 track.
■ Your track can only ever be as good as your baseboard. A good baseboard pays dividends in terms of the smooth running of your trains. MDF and plywood are two of the most popular baseboard materials, fixed on a light timber frame.
■ When using flexible track, a Tracksetta aluminium template is a worthwhile purchase to ensure that curves are laid smoothly. These templates are manufactured by Peco.
■ Paint the sides of the rails a rusty brown colour – real rails are never shiny! Acrylic paint and a fine paintbrush are all that are needed.
■ Use under-board point motors if possible. Point motors sitting on a baseboard do not look prototypical!
■ Buy one of the track cleaning rubber pads (from Peco or Squires) to keep the rails clean. It's best to hoover off the residual dirt once the rails are cleaned.

Terms

■ Underlay – A form of 'cushion' between the track and the baseboard which deadens the sound of passing trains and offers a smooth bed.
■ Set track – Pre-formed track, available straight, curved and with points, which is easy to use and simply slots together. Curves come in fixed radii.
■ Flexi-track – This type of track comes in yard lengths and can be used to form long straights or any curve required from a gentle sweep to a first radius return curve.
■ Points – Junctions which allow trains to change tracks.
■ Code 100/75 – Description of the rail height. Code 100 is the standard rail height and Code 75 is a fine scale variation.

Taking the shock out of electrics

Baffled by electrics? Confused by current? IAN MORTON has the answers in this guide to how model railway electrics work and the basics of common return wiring. *Illustrations, John Wiffen.*

Model railway electrics is a topic which makes otherwise rational people start to tremble and break out in a sweat. Many modellers say that they are baffled by the electrics under their layout or even can't build a layout because they don't understand how to wire it up. Fear not! In this section we will guide you through the basic principles of how a model railway works electrically and offer tips and techniques to make you a proficient model railway electrician.

The electrical knowledge and skills that you need to successfully wire up a model railway are limited and easy to acquire. Don't be fooled into thinking that because there are hundreds of wires beneath a layout that it must all be terribly complicated: it isn't. It is the same few simple circuits repeated many times over, but, depending on the size of your layout, it may need a lot of wire.

First we need some ground rules. Those of a technical disposition may well like to complicate the wiring of their model railway: that is their choice and something that they enjoy. If you are, or aspire to be a technical whiz kid, then you ought to join

the Model Electronic Railway Group (MERG), which caters for those of us who like playing with circuits – details can be found on their website *www.merg.org.uk*

For the rest us, we need some ground rules to ensure that life isn't complicated by model railway wiring and that the otherwise inevitable headaches over a fault are easier to deal with.

Rule 1. NO MAINS ELECTRICITY.

Buy a professionally-made power supply for your model railway and only use low-voltage (12V to 16V) outputs. Do not be tempted to run a mains cable along your layout. Mains voltage can, and does, kill. Don't take any chances with it; I'd hate to lose a reader!

Rule 2. USE THE CORRECT TOOLS.

I shall come back to this as I describe the tools that you need. Using the correct tool ensures that the task is done effectively and efficiently. As an example, use a wire stripper to strip the insulating sleeve off lengths of wire. Do not use a craft knife, however tempting it may seem. The knife may slip and cut you, but it is also more than likely to cut off some of the wire strands and lead to a weakened connection that may well fail at a later date.

Rule 3. COLOUR CODE YOUR WIRING.

A simple colour code can make it much easier to work out what wire goes where. If your track feeds are all red for one side and black for the other it makes it much harder to introduce a short

circuit by connecting different rails together.

Rule 4. KEEP IT TIDY.

It is so tempting just to run a couple of wires 'to see if it works' and then a couple more until you have something that resembles a bird's nest under the layout. Keeping your wiring tidy will help you when it comes to locating faults or making changes.

Rule 5. KEEP NOTES.

Along with Rules 3 and 4 this is all about making future fault finding or amendments easy. You may know what the green and purple striped wire that you used (because you didn't have any of the correct colour) does now, but you won't remember when a length of track mysteriously goes dead in nine months time. Make sketches of the wiring, noting where the wires go and what they do. Ideally you should number each end of each wire with a sticky label so that if they are ever disconnected, either by design or accident, you can establish where they should go.

Electrical principles

Let's get started, and where better than with the locomotive? For the moment I shall assume we are looking at a standard 12V DC locomotive; it can be any scale or gauge. Inside is an electric motor connected to the track via the wheels (Diagram 1). For the purpose of this exercise we will assume there is a standard model railway controller connected to the track.

As we turn the knob on the controller from OFF to MAXIMUM the motor in the locomotive will

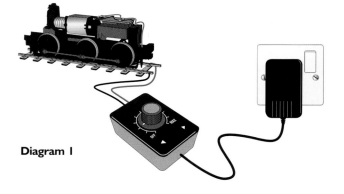

Diagram 1

Diagram 2

Diagram 3

run faster and faster. When we turn the knob back to off, the motor stops. If we then change the direction switch and move the knob again the motor runs in the opposite direction (Diagram 2).

The controller puts a VOLTAGE across the two rails. This is what causes the motor to run. As the voltage increases from 0 (OFF) to 12 (MAXIMUM) the motor goes faster. If we change the direction switch then the voltage is applied the other way around and goes from 0 (OFF) to -12 (MAXIMUM – in reverse).

A convention has arisen that the locomotive will move forward if the right-hand rail is positive and backwards if it is negative. This ensures that if two locomotives are being run by one controller they will both travel in the same direction.

If you lift the locomotive travelling 'up the page' off the track (Diagram 3), turn it around and replace it, it will carry on moving 'up the page' So if we have a controller connected to an oval of track and we put two locomotives on the track they will both run clockwise, or anti-clockwise, at the same time.

The problem with having two locomotives on the same track (Diagram 4) is that they both move at once and probably at different speeds. A common requirement on model railways is the ability to stop a locomotive responding to the controller.

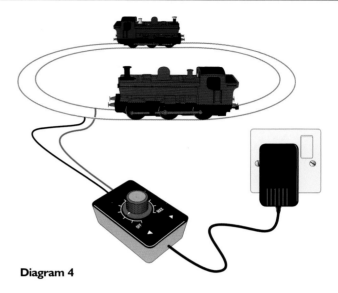

Diagram 4

To do this we need to use a switch. These are just like light switches, they can stop the electricity flowing to part of the layout and so stop any locomotives on that section responding to the controller.

Let's assume we now have two ovals of track (Diagram 45), with a locomotive on each. Both ovals are connected to the controller and both locomotives run at the same time.

If we put a switch in the red wire leading to the left-hand oval we can have both trains running if the switch is on, or just the right-hand train running if the switch is off. If we were to put another switch in the red wire leading to the right hand oval we could then choose to have either of the trains running on their own, both running at the same time or both stopped no matter how much we twiddle the controller's knob.

So, now we understand how to switch power to the track.

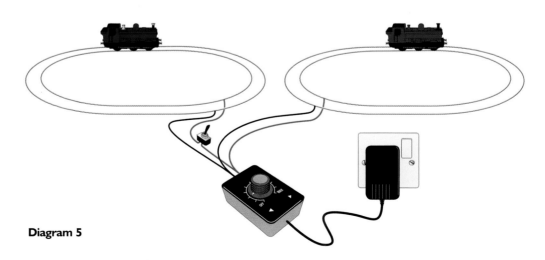

Diagram 5

The how to guides

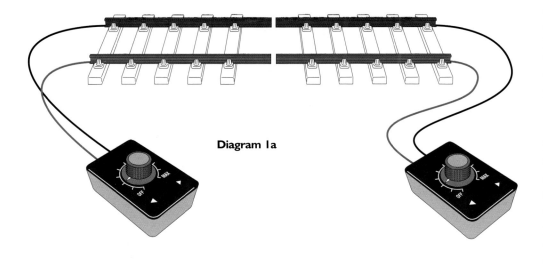

Diagram 1a

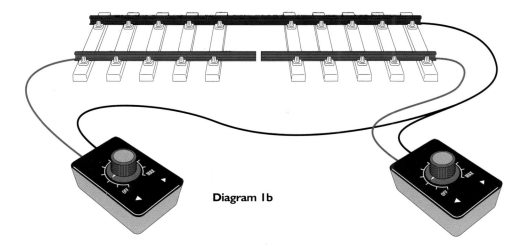

Diagram 1b

of each controller is connected directly to the 'black' rails on the layout, and the 'black' wires (the 'returns') are grouped together (in 'common') saving on wiring on the black side of the circuit (Diagram 1a and 1b).

You don't need any rail breaks in the 'black' rails (except for reversing loops and live-frog points) and you don't need any switches either. The only snag is that each controller must have its own mains plug. You cannot feed a number of controllers from one transformer and use common return wiring.

Switches

A simple 'on-off' switch can be used to isolate a locomotive by cutting off the power. This is normally known as a 'single throw' switch, often abbreviated to ST. Where the switch only has contacts to turn one wire on or off it is called a 'single pole' switch, abbreviated to SP. So, a single pole, single throw, or SPST, switch is a simple on-off switch.

Where the switch has contacts that can turn two separate wires on or off at the same time it is called a 'double pole' switch, abbreviated to DP. So, a DPST switch, a double pole single throw switch, will turn two wires on or off at the same time. This type of switch can be used to illuminate a light on the control panel at the same time as it supplies power to the track.

Common return wiring reduces the number of wires and overall complexity of the electrics on a layout with more than one controller.

Common return wiring

The switch is a probably the most useful component of standard DC model railway wiring. By using on/off switches we can isolate locomotives so that only one moves at a time. But what happens when we want to have two (or more) locomotives moving at once? Well, we need two (or more) controllers.

The snag is that we can't just wire a number of controllers to the rails and let them fight it out – this would result in overload cut-outs tripping and quite possibly some expensive, but short-lived fireworks.

We can connect different controllers to separate isolated sections of track, but that lacks flexibility and can lead to problems as trains pass from one controller's area to another. What we need are switches that can connect different

controllers to different sections of track.

Common return is a method of wiring up a model railway that can save money on switches and wiring. Basically each controller's 'red' wire is connected to the 'red' rails on the layout via whatever switches you need. The 'black' wire

When drawing out your circuit plans there are standard symbols to represent switches. The top symbol represents a single pole, single throw (SPST) switch and the bottom symbol represents a double pole, single throw (DPST) switch.

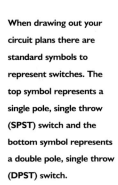

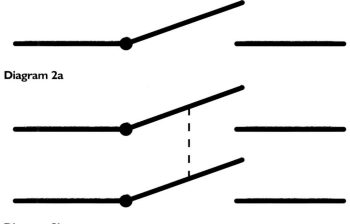

Diagram 2a

Diagram 2b

74   Hornby Magazine Yearbook

You could use a number of SPST switches to select which of a number of controllers is connected to a section of track. Apart from the cost this would also leave the problem that it would be possible to connect a section of track to more than one controller at once.

Changeover switches, also known as 'double throw' (abbreviated to DT) allow you to connect a wire to one of two connections. These switches can be used to select which of two controllers are connected to a section of track. As a bonus they are also available in 'centre-off' versions which have a central 'off' position where the track is not connected to either controller.

If you do not use common return wiring, then instead of a SPDT switch you will need to use a double pole double throw (DPDT) switch and wire the switch to both the red and black rails.

Switches come in various designs and sizes. The most common types used for model railways are toggle switches of various sizes and slide switches. Toggle switches are the easier of the two types to mount, just

needing a suitably sized circular hole drilling in a control panel (Diagram 4a and 4b) – which can be made from a section of plywood to suit your layout.

The practise
Imagine the simple layouts in Diagram 5a and 5b. It has two separate ovals and a goods yard so it is possible that three locomotives can run at once. Assuming that you are using common return wiring, by dividing the layout into ten sections, each fed from a SPDT centre off switch, you can operate three locomotives in a railway-like manner. By providing Sections 1 and 5 trains can be held in the tunnel which represents the rest of the railway system. Section 9 allows a locomotive arriving in the goods yard to be isolated whilst Section 10 serves the same purpose for the shunting locomotive.

For normal operation the inner loop would be operated by Controller 3, the outer loop by Controller 2 and the goods yard by Controller 1.

Now, imagine a clockwise freight ready to depart from the goods yard for a lap of the outer loop. The shunting locomotive would be

isolated in the headshunt (section 10) and the goods yard switched over to Controller 2 along with Sections 5, 6 and 7.

On arrival in section 7 the locomotive can run round its train using Sections 2, 3, 4 and 7. The train on the inner loop could be isolated in Section 1 whilst this takes place. Once the run-round is complete, Sections 1, 2, 3 and 4 could be switched back to Controller 3 for an anti-clockwise run of the train on the inner loop.

Meanwhile switching Sections 8, 9 and 10 to Controller 1 allows the shunter to continue with its work.

With a few switches we have transformed a simple train set type layout into an operable model railway.

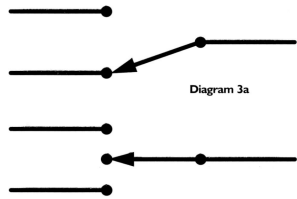

Diagram 3a

Diagram 3b

The top diagram is an SPDT switch that can be used to select between two controllers on a layout wired using common return. The lower diagram is a single pole, double throw centre-off (SPDT c/off) switch that can be used to select between two controllers and also isolate the section of track.

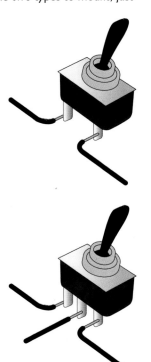

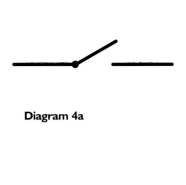

Diagram 4a

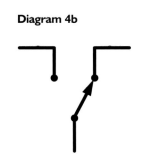

Diagram 4b

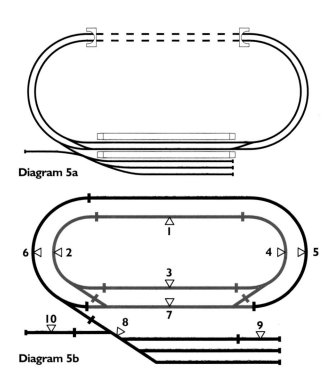

Diagram 5a

Diagram 5b

Building rolling stock from kits is a great way to expand your fleet. This is the Dapol 20-ton Class B tanker, assembled from a plastic kit.

The basics of plastic kit construction

Plastic kits have been a long standing part of model railways, but some shy away from building them. MIKE WILD provides tips and techniques for building plastic rolling stock kits and discusses why kit building is important. *Photography, Mike Wild.*

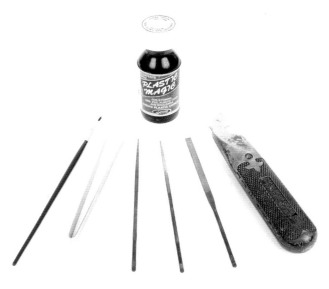

The tools you need – from left: a paint brush to apply liquid plastic cement, tweezers to handle small parts, needle files to clean up parts, a craft knife to separate components from sprues and liquid plastic cement to glue parts together. To finish a kit you will also need suitable paints a selection of fine paint brushes.

Ready-to-run models keep getting better and better and to some extent this is the first port of call for layout builders wanting to increase their fleet of rolling stock. But railway modelling should be about more than just collecting. It should be about learning techniques, model making and immersing ourselves in projects to while away an evening or two at a time.

The humble plastic wagon kit has been around almost as long as ready-to-run rolling stock. In fact, some of the products available through Dapol date back to the 1960s and Airfix, but, even so, they can still create good finished models with a little thought and care.

But why build a kit? Isn't it easier just to buy a ready-to-run item in a box? That way, at least we know for sure that the chassis will be square, that we won't get stuck half way through and that everything, even the tinyest detail, will be correct. Flipping the coin and a kit built goods wagon, the simplest of all rolling stock kits, will add a new dimension to a fleet, particularly if you choose a prototype which isn't readily available from the ready-to-run manufacturers.

There are many kit manufacturers out there. Some products are easy to build, other not so. The range produced by Parkside Dundas for example offers modellers a superb range of finely detailed goods wagon kits with clear instructions and good quality mouldings. Also as good, although not as finely detailed, is Dapol's range of goods wagons. Most of their range originated with Airfix.

Despite the age of the kit, and others in the range, they still make good models and they aren't difficult to assemble either.

For this guide to building plastic kits we've used the Dapol 20-ton Class B tanker – originally introduced in the 1960s by Airfix. The pictures show what to expect from a plastic wagon kit together with the dos and don'ts of kit construction.

The best advice we can offer is have a go. You'll be surprised how much pleasure it gives to assemble a kit and set it running on your layout and once you've tried your hand at a few, you'll soon be hungry for more complex projects!

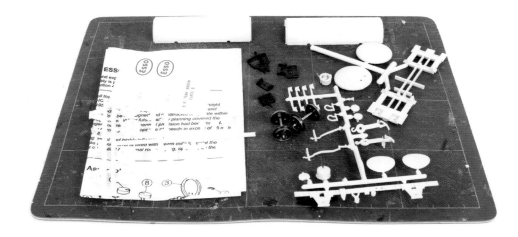

A classic plastic kit includes everything you will need to complete the job from instructions to body and chassis components, wheels, couplings and transfers. Some of the more advanced kits require transfers and couplings to complete, but all kits require paint to be bought separately.

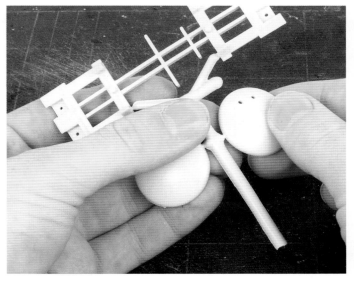

DON'T! Snap plastic components off their sprues, no matter how tempting it might be. You may damage the parts and make the kit more difficult to assemble.

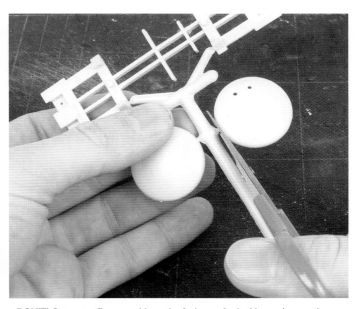

DON'T! Cut parts off sprues with a pair of scissors. Again this can damage the plastic of the actual part.

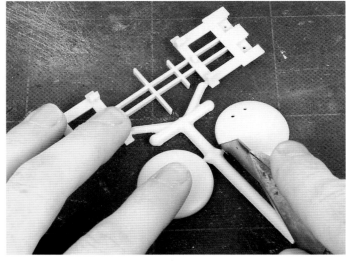

DO! Carefully remove parts from sprues by cutting through the mounting sprig with a craft knife. Any excess material can be cleaned up with a small file or emery board.

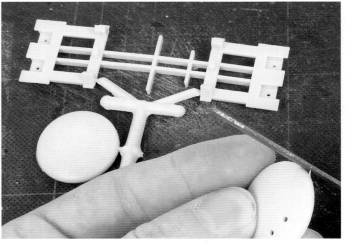

A set of fine needle files is very handy for building kits. Different shaped files allow you to get into various corners to clean up excess plastic from the moulding process – which is usually minimal. Each component needs to be checked over and cleaned up as necessary.

To assemble a plastic kit we recommend using a liquid plastic cement. This can be applied sparingly with a paint brush in the required areas and offers a neat way of fixing components together. Used here is Deluxe Materials Plastic Magic – *www.deluxematerials.co.uk*

A pair of tweezers is an essential part of any modellers' tool kit. They are great for jobs like this where small parts need to be fitted into tight spaces.

The finishing process for a plastic kit involves applying transfers. This vehicle has been given a coat of Railmatch Gloss Varnish, as transfers adhere to gloss varnish better than any other finish. It is then a case of cutting out the required transfer with a pair of small scissors, soaking it in water for a few moments, then sliding it into position on the vehicle. To finalise its position, use a paint brush to gently move the film then use kitchen paper to soak up excess water.

The very final process, before weathering if desired, is to spray the whole vehicle with a coat of Matt Varnish – we used Railmatch Matt Varnish. This seals the transfers and finish and offers a muted tone to the overall colours and also provides a key for weathering.

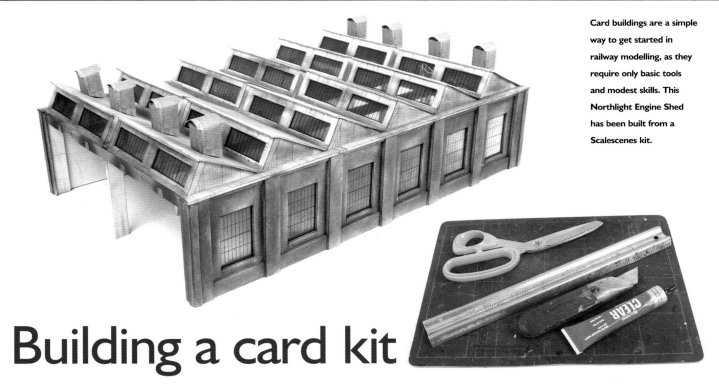

Building a card kit

For many years the card building kit has been the backbone of model railway buildings and structures. MIKE WILD takes on a Scalescenes kit and offers tips and techniques for the making the most of card construction. *Photography, Mike Wild.*

Card kits have been the backbone of model railway buildings and structures for many years. They come in all shapes and sizes from pre-cut flat packed versions such as Meltcalfe Models and Superquicks ranges to downloadable kits such as those produced by internet based company Scalescenes.com

Some will argue that card is outdated and doesn't offer the realism of a plastic kit, but, on the other hand, it is a sturdy material and requires a lot less finishing work than a plastic kit. For the home layout it is ideal.

Whichever type of kit you choose to build, there a few techniques that are worth knowing and certain tools and glues are required too and this is what we'll explain here – the basics of card kit construction.

Firstly, why build a card kit in preference to purchasing a ready-made building or a plastic kit? Ready-made buildings are great, and I'm the first to admit that they are the

simplest way of adding structures to a model railway. However, if you want to personalise your layout or you'd rather spend your cash on ready-to-run locomotives and rolling stock, then kit built buildings are a good direction to take.

Compared to a plastic kit, the key advantage is that card versions come ready finished – you don't need to paint brickwork or other small details and there will be less weathering to do too in most cases.

The pre-cut kits, such as those produced by Metcalfe and Superquick, are very simple projects, but most of the techniques explained here are relevant to these types of kit too. However, we've centred this project around a Scalescenes.com kit. Scalescenes kits can be downloaded from the internet, printed using a home PC and colour printer and, if you do go wrong, you can always re-print the affected section. Equally, if you are looking to build a row of terraced houses, you only have to download the kit once, making it

much cheaper to build substantial town scapes.

The keys to building a good model from a card kit is patience, the right tools, care and the right type of glue. With the wrong materials, you might end up in a mess and wondering why you started in the first place.

Starting small with a simple project is always a good plan too, particularly if you are completely new to model railways and card modelling.

Card kit manufacturers		
■ Metcalfe Models	*www.metcalfemodels.co.uk*	01729 830072
■ Superquick	*www.superquick.co.uk*	01297 631435
■ Scalescenes	*www.scalescenes.com*	See website

Keeping the wheels turning

Clean wheels, a free running mechanism and clean rails are all vital to keep your models running smoothly. MIKE WILD shows how to maintain your locomotives running characteristics using three basic techniques.

Clean wheels, clean rails and a clean layout are all you need for a good running model railway.

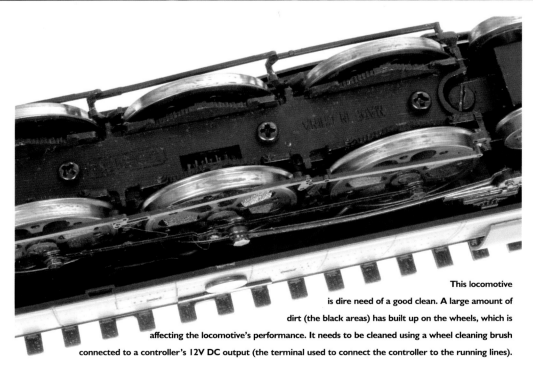

This locomotive is dire need of a good clean. A large amount of dirt (the black areas) has built up on the wheels, which is affecting the locomotive's performance. It needs to be cleaned using a wheel cleaning brush connected to a controller's 12V DC output (the terminal used to connect the controller to the running lines).

Good electrical continuity is important for smooth-running models. From time-to-time locomotives will need a little attention to keep them in tip-top condition as dirt and grease accumulates on the rails and transfers to the wheels of engines.

It is important to keep wheels clean, as dirt reduces the quality of the contact to collect electricity from the tracks. Just as important is an oiled mechanism as this will keep the gears and motor running smoothly and reduce friction. However, just to confuse the issue, some new models are essentially sealed units that should rarely, if ever, need oiling. The best practise here is always to refer to the instructions included in the box of each locomotive and, if you are in any doubt, contact your local modelshop for assistance.

There are a couple of essential tools that every model railway owner should have: a wheel cleaner, rail cleaner and specialist locomotive oil. All of these products should be available from your local model shop and no layout owner, no matter how small or big your project is, should be without these basics. Clean wheels and rails really do make a difference and will also help you enjoy your hobby more as locomotives will run properly without stalling on point work or other dirty sections of track.

Peco produces a useful wheel cleaning brush and scraper which can be connected to the 12V DC output on a controller. The current flows through separate wires (one to a brush and one to a scraper) and by touching the brush on one set of wheels and the scraper on the opposite set, the wheels rotate when the control knob is turned and the brush removes any dirt. There are alternative wheel cleaners including rail-mounted versions from the likes of Trix.

Rail cleaners are a common product and are available from Gaugemaster, Hornby and Peco ranges, as well as others. They look more like pencil rubbers than anything else. These 'rubbers' are hand operated and you simply rub the rail cleaner over the top of the rails to remove any grease or dirt. Be careful around point blades, as some rail rubbers do deteriorate over time and debris can work its way into the point blades and reduce the conductivity.

Another consideration for good running is general cleanliness of a layout. If it is covered in dust and hair, models won't run particularly well. All you need to do is to carefully vacuum the layout every once in a while – once a month should do – and it will keep the surfaces free from dust and other debris

The photographs show how the equipment is used.

To clean the wheels simply turn the locomotive upside-down and, with the brush and scraper connected to the positive and negative outputs on a controller, touch the brush on one set of wheels and the scraper on the other. Turn the control knob to send power to the brush and scraper, and hey presto, the wheels will rotate and become clean as the brush rubs off the dirt.

This model has also run dry of oil, so it needs freshening up with fresh oil. Only use specially-designed products to oil your models, as some not designed specifically for use with models can damage the gears. It is also important not to over-oil a model. Only ever add small amounts of oil to gears and never flood the mechanism with oil – two or three drops will normally do the trick.

Rail cleaning is a simple but essential task. Using a rail rubber, (this one is made by Gaugemaster) place it on the rails and apply a little pressure whilst moving it along the rails. Be careful around points, as these are easily damaged if too much pressure is applied when the rubber passes over.

Weathering a steam locomotive

A popular past-time is weathering of locomotives and rolling stock to give them a more realistic and used appearance. PAUL MARSHALL-POTTER tackles the Hornby 'M7' and shows how simple techniques can be used to create that all important 'used' look.
Photography, 2012 Images.

I n this piece we'll look at the basic principals of weathering a ready-to-run steam locomotive. Weathering is often seen as a 'black art', but with a few simple techniques it can make the difference between a good looking pristine model and a realistic finished project which looks like it has been hard at work.

For this project we've used a Hornby Dummond 'M7' 0-4-4T model – surely one of this manufacturers best ready-to-run steam locomotives.

Simple tools are all that's required: small files, a razor saw, small screwdrivers and good quality paintbrushes. For the 'M7' we also employed the use of a very simple airbrush, just to tone down the colors. The paints used are typical hobby colours, either from the Humbrol enamel range or Tamiya's acrylic range, and they are readily available from good hobby shops.

The only gloss shade used is the Humbrol clear varnish from spilt fuel and water, the rest are matt. The artists pastels are either Rowney or Winsor & Newton, and only four or five colors are needed, black, white, and three browns ranging from a bright orange bias to an earth brown and a bauxite colour. These, when mixed, will give a comprehensive range of shades and colors, and should meet all requirements. These same paints and pastels have also been used for the diesel project on the next pages.

The thing to realise is we're trying to replicate in miniature what happens/happened in the environment, so try to work from pictures of similar locomotives or vehicles to reproduce the 'wear and tear' in the pictures.

As such these example are generic examples of weathering from multiple sources, rather than a strict copy of a single example.

The model is out-of-the-box, and is an un-weathered release by the manufacturer concerned.

The Hornby 'M7' makeover
In this makeover we'll be looking at how to add everyday work staining to a steam locomotive using the Hornby 'M7' 0-4-4T as an example. It is an excellent model to start with and there is very little work to be done in terms of detailing. The only addition we'll make is the addition of real crushed coal in the bunker. The rest will be simply using paint and pastels to create the desired effect.

Our first task is to take the body off as we'll do two stages, chassis and body, and then bring them together. Follow the instructions in the box to remove the body. There are two screws, one underneath the bogie, and the other at the very front underneath the reservoir/tank which needs to be gently removed with a screw driver.

The Hornby 'M7' 0-4-4T was our chosen candidate for this weathering project. The finished result speaks for itself.

Step 1

To help paint key onto the coupling rods, take a glass fibre brush or wet and dry paper, and give the rods a gentle brush/rub over. This will provide fine scratches which the overcoat of paint will latch onto. Using Tamiya Nato black, XF69, or a very dark grey, brush paint the chassis, including the wheels, but make sure you don't get the paint on the wheel treads. Take your time with this as any 'clean' area will stand out like a sore thumb!

Step 2

I also use this Tamiya Nato black, XF69, to paint the smokebox. The smokebox was an area that got very hot, and discolored quickly in relation to the boiler and the rest of superstructure and this makes a big difference to a ready-to-run model.

Step 3

This is the chassis having been brush painted. The matt black areas are ready for a very light coat of Tamiya German grey, which will give a muted toning down of the chassis.

Step 4

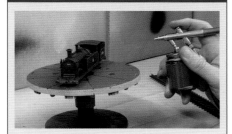

The body now gets the same treatment. All we are doing is providing a fine misting over the body using Tamiya German grey and along the cab roof and boiler. This gives a muted effect on the models base color, and a key for the pastels to grip to.

Step 5

It's important to observe the effects from prototype pictures that you want to replicate. Here we're using plain white pastel to simulate limescale deposits. On 'M7's' around the 1950s and into early '60s, the deposits were relatively small, and indeed stayed that way. However, if you were doing a Stanier '8F' 2-8-0 or a Riddles '9F' 2-10-0 from the northwest in the latter years, there would be significant amounts of limescale, and these were highly visible. So do work from reference photographs, it'll ensure a better model in the end.

Step 6

Turning attention to the smokebox, we're using some browns and rust colours to give a bit of warmth in terms of colour to the front end, again paint would peel from here due to the heat, so this area will show that effect. It's also where the smokebox was emptied, so there will be grey ash deposits too on the front footplating.

Step 7

Use the same earthy browns to replicate brake dust around the brakes and also around the ashpan where, like the smokebox, heat takes its toll! After this reunite the body and the chassis.

Step 8

Another way of looking 'in use' is to reproduce water spills, here we're using a gloss varnish and making it look like a splash from an overfill of the water tank. Don't overdo this though, too thick and it'll look wrong. You can use the same technique to replicate fuel and oil spillage and leaks on diesels.

Step 9

The final touch, real coal ground up and placed on a bed of PVA makes a big difference to the moulded coal as supplied. That's all it takes to make a simple yet very effective transformation to an out of the box ex-works locomotive! The elements to remember are, work from 'real life' images, build it up gradually, and keep looking back to the references as you work.

Weathering a diesel locomotive

Diesel locomotives offer great opportunities for weathering including details such as fuel spills and general grime. PAUL MARSHALL-POTTER provides a guide to weathering diesel locomotives using a ViTrains Class 37 as the basis. *Photography, 2012 Images.*

The finished model showing the range of weathering processes. This Class 37/0 is a ViTrains model and it has also been improved by the addition of etched BR double arrows underneath the drivers' window on each cabside.

When I saw a ViTrains class 37, there were several things that struck me on its appearance. There was a clear lineage back to Lima, ViTrains predecessor, but the chassis was a massive improvement and the paint finish was excellent.

Most manufacturers offer a version of their models in a weathered scheme, ViTrains, to date, (late summer 2008) are yet to do so. What they have done though, is introduce a wide range of liveries of this very popular locomotive and, so far three different sub-class variations – the 37/0, 37/3 and 37/4, all of which had subtle detail differences.

For this project there was a good choice of color schemes to choose from ranging from BR Railfreight red stripe, to triple-grey sector schemes, EWS maroon and gold and DRS blue. In some quarters of the hobby this model is overlooked, and I was interested in how it would 'scrub up' with a little effort. With this makeover, I have used an airbrush, but a very basic twenty plus year old Badger-200, just to give an overall dusting for the chassis, body and roof of the locomotive.

Having been given a free hand, a post sectorisation colour scheme was chosen, a scheme that would reflect the variations in effects that occur, and as they got grubby towards the end of their lives, would allow a complete variation in effects to be shown. I do work from images as a

rule, with this model I used three or four, and this shows a generic weathering pattern rather than a specific locomotive.

Although I've based this project on a more modern livery, the processes and techniques can be applied to any diesel locomotive from any period, whether that's an early BR green locomotive, a BR blue version or any other. The simple fact is that this particular livery shows up weathering rather well for photographs!

One thing that isn't included in the detail kit with the ViTrains 37 is etched BR double arrows. These are quite prominent on the prototype, underneath the drivers window on each cabside, and make an immediate difference to the model. Fortunately Steve at Geoffrey Alisons' in Worksop was able to supply a set from his personal stock with the locomotive, Cat No.V2038, 37201 in Triple Grey Metals scheme, to allow me to get started. The etched arrows are available in the Shawplan and Fox Transfers ranges.

How it started: From the box the ViTrains Class 37 provides a good candidate for a little details and it is often overlooked by modellers. However, the chassis inside is powerful and smooth running and, to boot, there are a large number of livery variations available.

Step 1

The biggest, and perhaps simplest, improvement is to paint the wheels black, to do this you need to remove the bogies, with a gentle flexing of the ends of the bogie frame the bogie sides will fall away. Using matt black paint, brush paint the wheel faces, but make sure you don't get any paint on the wheel treads. Whilst the bogie frames are off, paint those matt black too, I generally use Halfords matt black acrylic spray paint. Once dry refit the bogie frames and now it's on to the body work.

Step 2

Make up a thin matt black wash, using paint thinners and matt black paint, and apply it to all the panel lines and grills, and around the external framing too. This has to be a very thin pale wash, too thick or dark over accentuates the detail in the body and chassis we need to bring out.

Step 3

Using a home made paint mix, close to the base color of the model, I then used a piece of sponge to dab the color across the sector marks, around the etched arrows and across the body. This gives an appearance of patched repairs, deteriorating paint and vinyl decals. Don't over do this, the key is restraint. You can also reduce the brightness of the sector logos, by drawing the sponge vertically down the vinyl, leaving a very faint trace of paint, which tones the color down significantly.

Step 4

The whole locomotive has now had a very light overspray of Tamiya German Grey, XF63, for the roof and Flat Earth, XF52, for the chassis. The paint/thinners ratio is about 70:30 as we are literally toning down the factory colour. Here I'm starting to work ground up artist's pastels onto the body work. I use a few colors, black, white, mid earth brown, and two rust colors. One an orange, and the other a bauxite type color. Grinding small amounts of these on coarse sandpaper will give plenty of material to use and plenty of colour variation too.

Step 5

Build the colour up gradually, if you apply too much at this stage it is almost impossible to recover it, so build it up gently, and work across the body so it all builds up as 'one'. You can always go back to rework an area if need be.

Step 6

Using a very light wash, put just a small dab of paint in a gutter area of the edge of a grill. Before it dries you can smear it to give the effect of a spilt or dried run of liquid. Try this on a scrap piece before going ahead on a model, if you don't get the orientation correct, i.e. vertical or horizontal as required, it will look completely out of character and spoil the model.

Step 7

Here I'm re-working some of the streaks, by adding with this soft brush, plain black powders. The paint from the streaks is virtually dry, but there's enough residual dampness to catch some of the pure black and give a very recent and thick spillage look.

Step 8

Once happy with the overall finish, there are little touches that can really enhance and finish the model off. Here I'm applying scuffs on the steps with aluminium paint, areas that would wear to the natural metal under the paint, but wouldn't corrode due to continued wear and useage. I've already placed one or two small touches of rust around panels and join lines, but beware of these, too many and the locomotive will end up looking like a basket case on a scrap line. You can also simulate fuel spillages on the tank sides with a gloss varnish. This shows as up very well, but fuel costs money, so again restraint is the order of the day!

Step 9

The final task is to varnish the model. Some do, some don't. It will alter the weathering subtly as you are putting another coat of light reflective and absorbing material. I very rarely apply a top coat of varnish, as my models are not frequently handled, if yours are, it's definitely worth considering.

Basic freight stock weathering

If you've visited an exhibition lately or read a model railway magazine, chances are you'll have seen a rake of dirty freight stock. IAN FLEMING describes his simple methods for weathering goods wagons of 'planked' and 'steel' construction.

The term 'weathering' can mean many things to many people, but essentially encompasses a range of visual effects that help create an illusion of reality, and thereby enhance the realism provided by today's excellent models.

The two processes described here rely on a simple 'paint on, wipe off' process utilising washes of warmish greys and browns. It's based very much on how I started many years ago and although hardly the last word, it's a technique which once mastered will provide a sound basis for further development. The wagons used here are typical of the many excellent and readily available models in the ready-to-run ranges, and the work involves no major

repainting or use of transfers. Having said that, even though such models are not expensive, for a novice's first steps down this road a couple of old ex-swapmeet models will serve just as well with which to gain confidence.

Whatever techniques you follow (and there are many), bear in mind that you're not following some infallible 'recipe' that will guarantee success. You can't acquire experience and judgment in any other way than by experimenting for yourself. Start off with a fairly limited range of colours; although suggestions are given here, precise shades aren't too important and a little mixing will open up the scope of what you can do. Conduct trials with your materials, varying particularly the

amount of thinners in the wash and see how that affects workability and the final effect. Above all, remember that most effects owe much more to how you work and layer the paint than to using any supposedly 'correct' colours.

Any complex task becomes easier if you can split it into smaller stages, so the photographs lean towards a modular approach, broken down according to the construction of the vehicle. Work in short sessions and with small amounts of paint – don't try and do it all in one hit.

Although presented here as they have been applied to two distinct vehicles, remember that the modular basis means that such basic treatments can be applied to different types of wagon.

The finished vehicle, giving that indefinable but recognisable look of old, untreated wood; darker stains are supposedly from loads carried.

Weathering a wooden bodied wagon, step-by-step

Step 1

This Hornby model represents a typical five-plank open goods wagon in early BR bauxite livery. The excellent lettering should withstand anything short of deliberate annihilation, but if you're at all wary, a localised application of matt varnish (allowed to dry thoroughly) will protect it.

Step 2

Like many older models, a little preparatory work to remove mould parting lines will improve the finished job. Unclipping the couplings will make access easier.

Step 3

The first weathering task is to tone down the chassis and, already, this is giving the general look of an 'in service' wagon. This has been done with an overall dark brown coating of a mix of Humbrol matt black No. 33 and Chocolate No. 98. The precise mix can be varied with more or less of the black, but thin it only slightly, if at all – you're aiming to lose the 'plastic' look so it needs to cover (but not obscure) the detail, without being translucent.

Step 4

Moving on to the wagon body, much the same mix, albeit thinned down further, is applied and then wiped off straight away (ensure a ready supply of cotton buds, as you'll use a lot)! Work in small areas – ideally, don't apply more paint than you expect to be able to work before it starts to dry (although a little thinners will revive it again). I prefer a thickish wash – less than 50% thinners, as seen here – but the more cautious may wish to use something weaker, and build it up gradually.

However you apply it, it's essential to work with the detail. Get the mix into all the plank lines and corners – this is where dirt would naturally collect and/or where shadows would fall. The contrast between the three panels here shows something of the range of effects that can be obtained with different amounts of rubbing away.

Step 5

The finished side after a little more work. The above technique will have the effect of leaving the corner plates, door stanchions and other ironwork looking 'cleaned', so here they have been picked out with a rusty brown (Revell brown No. 84) applied with a small brush. Selected planks have also been drybrushed with the bodywork mix, to accentuate the careworn effect. Drybrushing is at the other end of the scale from a wash, and is where nearly all of the paint is wiped off the brush, leaving a small amount to be stroked over the surface of the model.

Step 6

A popularly sought effect, and particularly applicable here, is that of unpainted wood. There is no great mystery to achieving this, but it is essential to use several layers of paint; and as with everything, a little more time going back over certain areas will produce a more convincing effect. The basis, as seen being mixed here, is a light brownish/grey, in this instance from Humbrol Nos. 147 and 187.

When you're ready to move on, remember that observation is key to convincing weathering. Using photographs, analyse a vehicle's constructional features – which parts were wood, which were metal, where there are fittings that would get naturally grimed or abraded. Work with the detail, not against it, by getting into all those corners and crevices; and blend the elements of the finish together with light strokes to avoid stark, isolated blotches of colour. The aim is not necessarily just to produce something that looks filthy and decrepit, but to make your models look like they are actually made up of sheets of plywood, steel sections or whatever, and not a lump of injection moulded plastic.

Finally, take a long hard look at it when you've finished, admire your achievement – and go back over the little bits you've inevitably missed...

Step 7

Coat this mix over the interior, fairly thickly, but not necessarily evenly. I often save a little time by doing this straight after the chassis coating, as the two are quite separate and shouldn't interfere with each other. Having allowed it to dry thoroughly, the same dark brown coating used for the outer body is washed over it and worked with a cotton bud or paintbrush. A thinner wash is definitely called for here; probably two-thirds thinners – but don't work it too vigorously or you'll disturb the base coat!

The finished steel-bodied mineral wagon after some refining. To avoid a stark a contrast with the clear areas of livery colour, these have been filled in to some extent with various flecks, scores and smears, applied with a fine brush.

Goods wagons were almost always filthy, although ex-works vehicles would retain a clean appearance for a short time. Stanier '8F' 2-8-0 48322 rounds the curve to Woodley Junction with an empty coal train formed of steel bodied mineral wagons bound for Godley Junction, on 6 April 1968. Brian Stephenson.

Weathering a steel bodied wagon, step-by-step

Step 1

Rust is an infinitely varied effect, one which can be very absorbing and time consuming for the modeller. The finish to be applied to this model is a relatively easy way to achieve the characteristic flaky effect, yet without producing the 'camouflaged' appearance often so apparent on some models.

Step 2

Once again Revell paint No. 84 is useful, being a fairly subtle rusty shade. A word of warning here; most paints that you will buy described as 'rust' are far too bright for such large applications. The chassis has been coated in a similar way to the five-plank, although again, a little black in the mix wouldn't hurt, and the application continued fairly roughly to the body sides.

Step 3

Leave this at least a day to harden, then again line up your cotton buds. Moisten one end in thinners and wet a small area of the model, then use the clean end to lightly rub at the paint. For a less rusted wagon, rub harder, or start with a lighter application of paint.

Step 4

Done correctly, this should gradually remove some of the paint, leaving realistic rough edges and smaller flecks. Again the basic finish is fairly sound, but be careful around the diagonal white stripe – as you can see, I wasn't!

Step 5

The door end of the wagon is treated similarly but will probably require thinner paint and more brushwork. It's essential to get into all the detail, as any tiny factory-fresh patches will stand out and destroy the illusion.

Step 6

The inside of the wagon can be base-coated with a rusty brown (again at the chassis painting stage if desired). Take particular care to get an even coverage on the top edges of the body. Once dried, the interior can be dusted with a suitable weathering powder to vary the tone. Finally, the chassis has been lightly dusted with a further weathering powder to produce subtle highlights; oh, and it's had that white stripe painted in again!

Road vehicle makeover – the AEC Mercury

While rolling stock weathering is comparatively common, many forget to add that extra touch of realism to their model road vehicles. PAUL MARSHALL-POTTER explains how he made the most of Base Toys budget AEC Mercury flatbed and tanker lorries. *Photography, 2012 Images.*

The finished vehicles look the part of lorries that are used in service. These are both Base Toys AEC Mercury's – one a flatbed, the other a tanker.

The first thing to say is railway modelling can be dangerous. Not in an extreme downhill mountain biking kind of way, but you are going to be using sharp tools, things may break, and splinters may fly.

This makeover of the Base Models AEC tanker and flatbed brought that home to me with quite a shock.

Whilst prising the windscreen and cab interior out, the screwdriver slipped, shattered the windscreen, and snapped the blade which ricocheted around the workshop, yet to be found! It was a salutary lesson in taking care in the workshop, and eye protection.

Most of the work on these trucks is very easy to do, both were completed in an afternoons work. As they come they are a very high gloss, toy-like finish, but I recognised the potential immediately. They are very cheap, less than £5 each, so they must go together quickly and easily for production and therefore the reverse is true for modification!

Step 1

The first job was to remove the wheels from the chassis. As you can see I've used tweezers to lever them off, as these wouldn't unscrew. They are 'self-tappers' when fitted, some will unscrew, if they don't use the method above.

Step 2

Unscrew the cab from the chassis, you can also remove the body/tank if required.

Step 3

Using a screwdriver you can lever out the cab and glazing, it can take some force and effort.

Step 4

Gently lever the glazing out of the cab, this is where the blade snapped in the introduction. Again the amount of glue varies so expect some difficulty.

Step 5

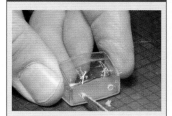

Open out the mounting holes in the cab roof, the glazing is held in place by the cab and floor. The scratches on the glazing will not be an issue as they will be replaced with flush glazing. To fit flush glazing, cut away the front of the moulded glazing unit with a razor saw or a similar tool – this job is optional.

Step 6

This is what the components will look like. Note the glazing has been tidied up with a file and the interiors have been painted with Halfords red plastic primer. I left one cab entirely open, side windows too, hence the 'L' shaped section in the foreground.

Step 7

Paint the interior and edges including window surrounds with matt black, at this point I'd paint any cab details too.

Step 8

Using a black wash, (very thinned paint), fill the panel lines and wheel trims, this makes an enormous difference to the finish.

Step 9

To improve the tank, remove the steps, and sand the ends so they are flush with no gaps.

Step 10

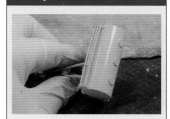

I used white Halfords Plastic primer, to get a good finish on the tank, and then chose a Halfords Ford Signal Yellow, as a typical tanker type colour. These are simple spray cans applied following the instructions on the can.

Step 11

To reglaze the cab, use a material such as Wills Scenics packaging, or a sheet of plastiglaze, hold it inside the cab, and gently score around the edge. You can then trim this close to the final shape required.

Step 12

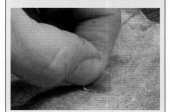

Using wet and dry paper, sand the glazing until you get interference fit in the aperature. This does take time and effort, but is worth it for the final appearance.

Step 13

For the tanker I found some decals from a 1/48th WWII P-47 Thunderbolt in the spares box, (don't throw stuff away, you'll always find a use for it), and applied them using the normal waterslide technique. I was after an appearance of typical stencils, you can actually read them if you look closely!

Step 14

The final items for assembly; note flush glazing, new transfers and colour scheme, lightly weathered cab and wheels. The hose in the side baskets of the tanker are made from electrical wire; this holds its shape once formed.

Engine Wood

Set in the early BR steam era on the Somerset and Dorset Railway Engine Wood appeared in the very first issue of *Hornby Magazine* and came joint fourth in *Hornby Magazine's* first layout of the year competition. *Photography, Chris Nevard.*

Sometimes circumstances change and a project has to be 'abandoned' in the early stages of a build. Of course this is a bad thing really, as no one really wants to give up their hobby, even temporarily, but in the case of Tim Maddocks evocative recreation of a might-have-been station on the former Somerset and Dorset Railway network, it was almost certainly a good thing!

This layout started life in 1976 with the original intention that it would be a Great Western Railway branch line set in the 1930s. Initially, the baseboards were built and some track was laid, but otherwise the layout stood idle waiting for its moment of glory. By the early 1980s and following two house moves, layout builder Tim Maddocks had progressed the scenery and made an important decision – to change the period from the 1930s to the early 1950s BR era.

This popular period has captured the hearts of many, but the Somerset and Dorset route offers something a little more special. For starters, the route was tremendously scenic – 'chocolate box' England, if you will. But the real attraction for modellers lays in the variety of motive power which traversed the route and its branches. Here you could find everything from Midland Region heavy freight classes such as Stanier '8F' 2-8-0s to mixed traffic engines from the Midland, Southern and BR Standard fleets as well as a smattering of ex-Great Western locomotives. In terms of variety it is second to none, except maybe the North London line which attracted inter-regional freights moving between the major marshalling yards around the capital.

Back to Enginewood. After the brief flurry of activity in the 1980s, the layout was packed away again until the summer of 1994. Tim takes up the story: "By this time my modelling preferences had shifted from the GWR/WR to the former Somerset and Dorset Railway (S&D), which ran from Bath Green Park station over the North Mendip hills

to evocatively named stations like Midford, Chilcompton, Evercreech Junction and Templecombe. Faced with an exhibition deadline at the end of 1994, I decided to use what I already had, rather than start completely from scratch and continued with the original boards from the initial GWR layout."

Enter Engine Wood

"The name 'Engine Wood' has its origins in the building and operation of the Somerset Coal Canal, which ran from Paulton Basin in the south of Bristol to the Dundas Aqueduct on the Kennet & Avon Canal, near Bath," Tim said. "This canal was constructed to transport coal from the Cam valley pits, south of Bath, to markets in Bath, Bristol and further afield.

"The GWR opened a branch from Hallatrow to Camerton in 1882 with an eye on the possibility of lucrative coal traffic from the collieries in the district. There had been various proposals to build a railway along the remainder of the Cam Valley

3 With a mixed group of box vans behind, an ex-LMS 'Jinty' 0-6-0T approaches Engine Wood.

2 Opposite page: A kit-built BR '3MT' 2-6-2T waits to run-round its train as a box van set departs in the opposite direction.

1 Previous page: A work stained BR 'Standard Five' 4-6-0 enters Engine Wood station with a short stopping train, typical of the early 1960s ex-Somerset and Dorset branch lines.

■4▶ Although steam is more common at Engine Wood, from time-to-time Tim breaks with tradition and operates early diesel classes including this 'Hymek' Bo-Bo.

■5▶ Standing outside the scratchbuilt station building, a BR '3MT' 2-6-2T pauses at Engine Wood with a pair of ex-GWR Collett coaches.

towards Midford and Limpley Stoke, but in 1910 the GWR decided to build the line from Limpley Stoke to Camerton.

"The historical raison d'être for the model, Engine Wood, however, requires that history deviates slightly from this account to propose that the Somerset & Dorset funded and built a line through the Cam Valley, running from Midford and making an end-on junction with the GWR at Camerton. It is assumed that the S&DJR managed to negotiate running rights over the GWR from Camerton to Hallatrow and eventually constructed a north-facing spur at this location, enabling them

to run through to Bristol Temple Meads without reversing."

With the change from the initial 1930s GWR branch line plan, Tim settled on the period between 1959 and 1964 for Engine Wood when the S&D was beginning to fade as closure approached. Filling in the background to the layout, Tim commented: "By this time private car ownership had started to increase and a lot of freight had been permanently turned away from the railways as a result of the general upsurge in road traffic, aided some say by the effects of the 1955 ASLEF strike.

"Consequently, local passenger trains would be running between Bristol Temple Meads and Radstock, with some going through to Evercreech Junction or Templecombe. Coal traffic is still at quite high levels from the remaining colliery at Camerton, which in this 'time line' has maintained healthy coal reserves and was extensively modernised by the NCB in 1955. Production looked to be guaranteed for many years to come with the coal going mainly to Portishead Power Station and to the various municipal gas works on the south coast. Local freight traffic is just hanging on, unlikely to last much longer."

Creating the scene

Tim used techniques described by scenery expert Barry Norman to create the landscape and features on Engine Wood. Tim said: "It must have been a real joy to travel along the real S&D line, especially in late Spring or early Summer through some of the finest countryside in England, and I have tried to recreate this atmosphere on the layout."

The shape and form of the landscape was created using card and fine chicken wire with several layers of newspaper soaked in a mixture of filler and white wood glue laid over the top. The 'paste' mixture also included brown powder paint to give an instant earth colour to the landscape. The finishing touch was another skim of the filler and glue mix before the future grassy areas were treated to a base colour wash of olive green. To achieve the realistic grass effects Tim used surgical lint dyed with Dylon 'Olive Green'. On top of this, and to add

further depth, Heki and Noch grass fibres were added over the top which stand on end and give the effect of long grass.

Tim takes up the story: "Most of the medium size trees on Engine Wood use the old Woodland Scenics whitemetal tree skeletons. I'm not sure if you can still get these, although I believe that plastic ones are available. Once again I applied the methods described by Barry Norman; in this case varying shades of foliage foam sprinkled onto clumps of rubberised horsehair.

Since making those trees, I have found that I prefer to use Heki foliage matting as the basis for leaf cover, and have re-foliated some of the trees with Heki material. The large elm and ash trees seen on the layout were scratchbuilt, with skeletons made from varying grades of copper wire, with masking tape covered with Polyfilla/PVA on the trunks and main branches. This has become my preferred method of making trees, although I have started using 'Seafoam' trees in recent years."

⑥ **A diesel shunter from the colliery pulls past the signalbox before leaving the 16-ton mineral wagons in the BR sidings.**

⑦ **As well as detailing the locomotives and rolling stock, Tim has invested a lot of time in the buildings and scenics.**

8 A '4F' 0-6-0 pauses between duties in the goods yard at Engine Wood.

9 The local bus service calls at the station to meet the latest arrivals.

Other scenic details include bushes and hedgerows made in a similar manner to the trees and wild flowers produced from short stands of sisal string. Clumped grass and weeds growing through the ballast have been added at the base of buildings using old carpet underlay or Heki puff grass.

"Most of the buildings on Engine Wood are scratchbuilt, such as the main station building, the platform shelter and the signalbox." Tim added: "I was able to use a Wills kit for the lock-up goods shed and a Ratio kit for the concrete Permanent Way hut. The signalbox was actually scratchbuilt by Simon Castens for his Camerton layout, but as it fitted my needs for Engine Wood, he was kind enough to loan it to me.

"The buildings and girder bridges are made from styrene sheet, whilst the station building has individual slate strips made of thin paper and the tunnel mouth was constructed from balsa with a plaster covering, onto which stonework has been scribed and then painted with watercolours. The signals are mostly built from M.S.E. components, although the Up Home signal has a scratchbuilt Southern Railway type rail-built post; operated by Seep point motors, mounted underneath the baseboards."

Operations – real and model

The operational side of Engine Wood is just as important to Tim as the scenery and buildings. "Merely sending trains from one fiddle yard to the other, with them passing each other at the station in both directions, is all too easy on a layout like Engine Wood," he said. "This is only possible, also, with a sufficient number of operators to keep the fiddle yards in a state of readiness. Consequently, shunting sequences seem an ideal alternative when there are fewer operators.

"The '6.05pm Bristol Temple Meads to Engine Wood' local imitates the 6.05am Bath to Binegar local on the real Somerset and Dorset line. This was latterly formed as a single coach, usually hauled by a BR '3MT' 2-6-2T, which ran round at the station before embarking on its return journey to Bath Green Park, usually empty. On Engine Wood a lack of paths on the S&D main line beyond Midford Junction means that trains have to run round at Engine Wood.

"An NCB shunting engine is involved in another operation, to transport loaded coal wagons from Camerton Colliery ('off stage') to the Exchange Siding at Engine Wood. This somewhat unusual practice has been sanctioned, in my fictional extract from the Sectional Appendix, by arguing that the poor condition of the track inside the colliery necessitates the banning of BR locomotives from entering the colliery. In practice this means that a small industrial locomotive and a rake of mineral wagons can be sent to the station, run round and shunted to the Exchange Siding, to be picked up later in the sequence by a main line engine such as the Fowler '7F' 2-8-0 or, perhaps, a 'Hymek' diesel hydraulic.

"I try to maintain scale speeds when operating the layout at exhibitions, especially when shunting, and it is interesting to remember that drivers of shunting engines did not always crawl along at a walking pace; they frequently opened their machines up and gave

the stock a clout, especially if they were in a hurry to get back to the depot and book off!"

The fleet for Engine Wood consists of a mixture of kit built and modified ready-to-run equipment. Most are weathered to one degree or another, as few steam locomotives were kept in pristine condition by the 1960s. The real S&D remained a 'steam only' line until the end, so that is what the majority of the fleet is – steam powered. On occasion though, early green diesels do appear on Engine Wood.

Tim has the last word: "For those of you who are wondering, Engine Wood is a real place, but it is not a real station. The real GWR line, from Limpley Stoke to Camerton, ran close to the real Engine Wood. At exhibitions I hang

a signalbox diagram of Engine Wood on the front of the layout. It was drawn by a real-life S&T engineer and he even gave it a serial number! This illustrates how far I was prepared to go back then to hoodwink the public into thinking that Engine Wood actually existed. I've actually had people tell me that they remember waiting on the platform for a train there…"

■ Tim would like to thank all the people who have helped him in this hobby and in particular his wife, Madeleine Sara, for her constant advice and support, his friends in the Scalefour 'Devon Riviera' Area Group and others who have given help, encouragement and advice. Finally, Tim would like to give a big 'thank you' to Chris Nevard, for his outstanding photography.

A Midland '3F' 0-6-0, a common performer on the Somerset and Dorset, prepares to restart from Engine Wood.

Engine Wood Track Diagram

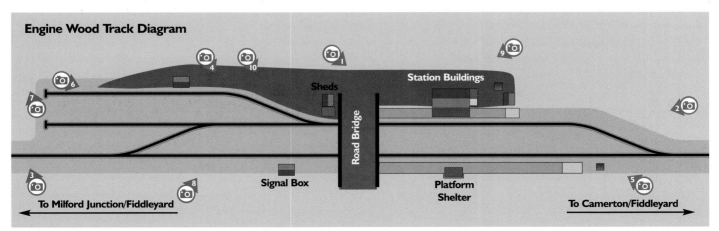

Sheds

Station Buildings

Road Bridge

Signal Box

Platform Shelter

To Milford Junction/Fiddleyard

To Camerton/Fiddleyard

The balance of power

British Railways inherited a colossal number of steam locomotive at nationalisation on 1 January 1948. KEITH GORDON shows how our model fleets can accurately represent BR's steam fleet using figures from 1955 and considers what ready-to-run locomotives are available.

Freight locomotives out-numbered express passenger machines on all of BR's regions, except the Southern Region. The Stanier '8F' 2-8-0s were on of the most numerous heavy freight classes. On March 4 1966, '8F' 48760 climbs out of Bath towards Devonshire tunnel, on the Somerset and Dorset route, with a train of coal empties for Writhlington Colliery. M Fox/Rail Archive Stephenson.

In a series of articles more than 30 years ago Don Rowland drew attention to the disparity between the locomotive and rolling stock rosters of many LMS model layouts and the reality shown by the official figures for 1938.

At the time I didn't pay much attention, but some years later I acquired my own set of figures from British Railways Book Stock of Locomotives, 1955, and realised just how much the real railway contrasted with the average modellers' perception. Consider for example, Class 8 passenger locomotives. The 'Top Link' express locomotives came to a total of 196,

and included many of the best known locomotive classes. Table 1 lists these eight classes in order of size.

All bar the last two of these are available as ready-to-run models, except that in 1955 the 'Merchant Navy' class were all still in their original condition, rather than the rebuilt form as produced by Hornby. The fact that the final two in the list are unavailable as ready-to-run models, ex-LNER 'W1' 4-6-4 60700 and BR '8P' 4-6-2 71000 Duke of Gloucester, is simply because they were unique locomotives which were never perpetuated.

However, these figures did not alter over the next few years, so if

you want Class 8 power on your passenger trains these are the options. In reality they would have been found hauling almost exclusively 10 to 15 vehicle expresses on the main lines. If you want to reflect reality on your model, you may have to forgo the pleasure of '8P' locomotives, or model the last years of steam, when, filthy or neglected, they were relegated to almost any duty.

At the opposite end of the glamour spectrum were the Class 8 freight locomotives whose numbers indicate a huge volume of freight. It is hard today to imagine how many freight locomotives were employed on BR or how rapidly the number of '8F' locomotives had grown as a result of wartime production. Stanier's '8F' 2-8-0, introduced in 1935 by the LMS, was chosen for wartime priority and virtually every available works was started on a massive build programme, and not just on the LMS – the GWR works at Swindon and even the SR's works at Ashford turned over to production of Stanier's '8F'.

At the start of the Second World War in 1939, around 100 had been built; by the end of the war, nearly 700 more had left the production lines. The figures included many which went overseas and which did not return for some time, if at all. In spite of this huge building programme, the ministry of supply wanted more easy to supply and cheaper to build heavy freight locomotives and Riddles, seconded from the LMS, obliged with his 2-8-0 and 2-10-0 'Austerity' designs. The latter only amounted to 25, although more were built for overseas service, which were all allocated to BR's Scottish Region, but in contrast 733 'WD' 2-8-0s were constructed.

The bulk of the 2-8-0s, despite being built for a short life, survived until the last years of steam. The full range of '8Fs' is listed in Table 2 ranging from the pioneering Churchward '28XX' 2-8-0s to the 'standard' Stanier '8F'.

To this total we can justifiably add GWR '52XX' and '5205' 2-8-0T classes and the GWR '72XX' 2-8-2Ts, 60 and 54 respectively, and also the BR '9F' 2-10-0s of which 70 had so far been built in 1955 of an eventual total of 251. This brings the heavy freight locomotive total to nearly 10 times the Class 8 passenger total.

The pre-dominance of freight locomotives was maintained throughout British Railways, if not to such a dramatic extent. Overall the distribution of BR locomotives was around 50% freight, 36% mixed traffic and 14% passenger, which makes a ratio of 7:5:2. If you have 14 locomotives, then that is how

they should roughly be arranged to reflect British Railways motive power fleet.

A slightly more useful measure would be to apply the same process to each of the six regions – BR's Western, Southern, Midland, Eastern, North Eastern and Scottish Regions – as shown in Table 3.

All the regions follow the same pattern as BR, with passenger locomotives having the smallest total, freight the largest and mixed traffic in the middle, except the Southern Region which manages to be completely different with freight locomotives the smallest and mixed traffic the largest.

This reflects the situation on the Southern. With no large industries – just the small Kent coal field and Southampton Docks to provide freight flows above the normal – and three major sources of passenger traffic: London commuters, overseas travellers and seasonal holiday traffic.

The remaining five regions broadly follow the pattern with passenger locomotives forming between an eighth and fifth of the individual regions total locomotive stock.

Reality and the model

Now we have some idea of the relative numbers of locomotives, it is time to look at which locomotives would be suitable on a model. Firstly, it is up to you what you run on your railway, but it does seem odd to spend so much money on buying locomotives which are as accurate as possible, and then not use them in a reasonably prototypical manner. Unless you model a main line, it is going to be hard to justify Class 8 power, but there are such nice models available it is tempting to justify them. Alternatively, there are many good models in the lower power ranges, perhaps more suitable for the model railway.

We can now look at the regions using the same percentage criteria, but only including locomotives available ready-to-run. I'll consider the regions in the same order as the BR list of 1955.

The London Midland Region

The largest of the six BR Regions, the London Midland, was the old LMS shorn of its Scottish lines, but otherwise mainly intact. Passenger locomotives were mostly tender designs (Table 4) – there were only 56 passenger tanks and none is available ready-to-run.

The passenger tender locomotives offer many ready-to-run models. The largest class is the Stanier 'Jubilee' 4-6-0, classified '6P'. There are 159 of these making 29% of the passenger locomotives and it is available again from Bachmann, having been reintroduced in December 2007.

Next in size is the standard '2P' 4-4-0 at 120 locomotives and 21.8% of the fleet. This class is available from Hornby. Hornby did produce another 4-4-0, the '4P' compound, with 102 in the class making 18.6% of the total. Both these models are of the older tender drive type and unless new versions are produced they will eventually only be available on the second hand market.

Hornby also produce the final passenger tender class of any significance, the rebuilt 'Royal Scot' 4-6-0, which entered the range in 2007 as a new highly-detailed model. The entire class of 66 was rebuilt by 1955, the last of the original Fowler

Table 1 – Class 8 passenger tender locomotives	
■ LNER/BR Peppercorn 4-6-2	50
■ LMS Stanier 'Princess Coronation' 4-6-2	38
■ LNER Gresley 'A4' 4-6-2	34
■ GWR 'King' 4-6-0	30
■ SR 'Merchant Navy' 4-6-2	30
■ LMS Stanier 'Princess Royal' 4-6-2	12
■ LNER rebuilt 'Hush-hush' 'W1' 4-6-4	1
■ BR '8P' 4-6-2 *Duke of Gloucester*	1
■ Total	196

Table 2 - Class 8 freight tender locomotives	
■ Riddles 'WD' 2-8-0	733
■ LMS Stanier '8F' 2-8-0	633
■ GWR Churchward '28XX' and Collett '2884' 2-8-0	167
■ LNER Gresley 'O2' 2-8-0	66
■ LNER Thompson (rebuilt Robinson 'O4') 'O1' 2-8-0	58
■ Riddles 'WD' 2-10-0	25
■ NER Raven 'Q7' 0-8-0	15
■ Total	1,727

The BR Western Region had only two dedicated express passenger classes, and the Collett 'Castle' 4-6-0s accounted for 75% of the fleet. 'Castle' 4083 *Abbotsbury Castle* passes Chester No. 6 signalbox as it leaves the town with up express in the 1950s.

J Mills/Rail Archive Stephenson.

design being completed during the year. They comprise just 12% of the LMR passenger total. Hornby also offer the similar rebuilt 'Patriot', but at only 18 examples, a tiny 3.3%, they are out-numbered by the 34 unrebuilt 'Patriots'. Interestingly, Hornby do produce this class as well, but it is let down by being paired with an over-width tender. Bachmann is working on a new model of the 'Patriot' which will fill a gap in the LMR fleet.

The mixed traffic locomotive had become increasingly popular with all companies as the economic benefits became clear. Initially, the 2-6-0 'Mogul' was the preferred type, but later 4-6-0s became the most popular and numerous; none more so than the LMS 'Black Five' 4-6-0 which was the second largest class of locomotive on British Railways.

The 842 members of the class were not all on the LMR, but 567 were, making them 54% of the region's mixed traffic tender locomotives.

The remaining mixed traffic classes available can be summarised as in Table 5. Half of these locomotive classes have only been produced in recent years, which is surprising, given how useful the mixed traffic locomotive is to the modeller.

The mixed traffic tanks of the LMR are of particular relevance in this regard. Table 6 lists the classes and their ready-to-run counterparts.

Now that they are all available it is worth giving the details. First built were the Fowler 2-6-4Ts introduced in 1927 with Fowler's trademark parallel boiler. In total 125 were built between 1927 and 1934, the final 30 receiving a side window cab.

Hornby's model dates back some time, but it was updated with a new chassis and released into the 'Super Detail' range a couple of years ago. Currently, the model is in the catalogue with a new chassis, which has also been used under Hornby's new Stanier 2-6-4T model which was first released in December 2007.

We now come to the Fairburn version, and this is where confusion sometimes arises. The Fairburn chassis was shorter by 1ft 5in over buffers. The Fairburn 2-6-4T was the first post-Stanier design reflecting the changing post-war world, a process which Ivatt would continue and which put the LMS at the forefront of British locomotive development. With ex-LMS man Robert Riddles appointed to the new BR as Chief Mechanical Engineer, the LMS influence continued. While work began on designing the standard classes, further construction of the Fairburn and Ivatt designs continued under BR for several years.

Table 3 - Passenger, mixed traffic and freight locomotive ratios

Region	WR	SR	LMR	ER	NER	ScR
Passenger	4	10	1	1	2	4
Mixed traffic	14	11	3	3	4	9
Freight	17	9	5	4	7	10

The Western Region kept its locomotives to itself, but the LMR was happy to see its new locomotives working on other regions, in effect they became the forerunners of the BR Standards.

The Fairburns, in particular, found their way onto all other regions except the Western, and their success led directly to the BR 'Standard Four' 2-6-4T 80000 series, although these had tapered side tanks to fit the BR composite loading gauge.

Table 7 shows how the London Midland Region's freight locomotives have been represented in model form. The most recent addition is Bachmann's recently announced model of the ex-LNWR 'G2a', or 'Super D', which was released within days of this Yearbook closing for press. Also available to represent LMR freight locomotives are the Stanier '8F' 2-8-0 and Fowler '4F' 0-6-0 from Hornby and the 'WD' 2-8-0 from Bachmann.

There is no need for a freight tank table since only one is available ready-to-run and that is the 3F 'Jinty' which both Hornby and Bachmann have produced. Anyway, with 434 members of the class amounting to 69% of the freight tanks the remaining 18 classes were relatively small and elderly. This pattern of tank engines being older reflects the unchanging freight working practices.

The Western Region
The Western had only 420 passenger locomotives (see Table 8a and Table 8b) and it is reasonably well represented. One further tank might interest the manufacturers. There were 40 passenger tanks in the '64XX' 0-6-0PTs class, which were push-pull fitted and a further 50 identical non-fitted '74XX' 0-6-0PTs, the final 10 of which were built in 1950. Though not push-pull fitted, these '74XX' class '2F' tanks could be found on passenger trains as well as freight and would make a useful alternative to the '14XX' 0-4-2Ts working light branches.

Western Region mixed traffic classes (Table 9) were more

numerous and well served by the manufacturers. Everybody calls them Collett Goods, but the '2251' 0-6-0s are given a mixed traffic title by the BR list and in the ABC, so are another useful branch line locomotive. The Collett 'Manor' 4-6-0 class was a particularly small class, but they have been very popular with modellers. The 'Grange' 4-6-0 class shared the same chassis and Hornby produces a fine model of this mixed traffic class.

The mixed traffic tanks (Table 10) are also well served by the ready-to-run trade, but a few notes are needed on these classes. The '56XX' 0-6-2Ts were originally built for coal traffic in South Wales and most remained there although a few did operate in other parts of the region.

The 'Large Prairies' were all rather similar. Officially the Hornby model is a '61XX' 2-6-2T, but the '81XX' had wheels only two inches less in diameter and the '5101' 2-6-2Ts had just a lower boiler pressure. The 'Small Prairies', the '45XX' and '4575' 2-6-2Ts are also virtually the same, differing only in the side tanks

and both are available from Bachmann.

There was only one freight tender locomotive of any significance on the Western and that was the Churchward '28XX' 2-8-0. Hornby produce this model which represents the Churchward design, whose 84 members make 25% of the region's total. If Hornby could produce the Collett side window cab they would also cover the other 83 members of the '2884' class. All other significant freight tender locomotives on the Western Region were LMR visitors. There were 47 'WD' 2-8-0s, 42 Stanier '8F' 2-8-0s and 27 'G2a' 0-8-0s.

In the lower power classes, tanks ruled and the only model available, forming 59.3% of all freight tanks, is the '57XX' 0-6-0PT. Both the original '57XX' and the later '8750' variant are available from Bachmann. There were 329 of the former and 523 of the latter, making this, numerically, the largest class on British Railways. This total of 852 is 11 less than the 863 usually quoted, but these 11 were the '97XX'

The BR 'Standard Four' 2-6-4Ts were the ultimate go-anywhere steam locomotive and they could be seen from the South Coast to the highlands of Scotland. 80093 climbs through Glen Ogle with the 4.05pm Callendar to Killin school train in June 1963. W Verden Anderson/Rail Archive Stephenson.

The balance of power! An ex-LNER 'A3' class 'Pacific', 60093 *Coronach*, passes Craigentinny carriage sidings with a Carlisle to Edinburgh Waverley express in August 1959. On the right mixed traffic Thompson 'B1' 4-6-0 61007 *Klipspringer* waits with empty coaching stock bound for Edinburgh Waverley. W Verden Anderson/Rail Archive Stephenson.

Table 4 – Ready-to-run LMR passenger tender classes

Locomotive	Number	%	RTR
■ Stanier 'Duchess' 4-6-2	29	5.3	Hornby
■ Stanier rebuilt 'Royal Scot' 4-6-0	66	12.0	Hornby
■ Ivatt rebuilt 'Patriot' 4-6-0	18	3.3	Hornby
■ Fowler parallel boiler 'Patriot' 4-6-0	34	6.2	Bachmann
■ Stanier 'Jubilee' 4-6-0	159	29	Bachmann
■ Fowler '4P' 4-4-0	102	18.6	Hornby (obsolete)
■ Fowler '2P' 4-4-0	120	21.8	Hornby

Table 5 – Ready-to-run LMR mixed traffic tender classes

Locomotive	Number	%	RTR
■ BR 'Britannia' 4-6-2	10	1	Hornby
■ LMS 'Black Five' 4-6-0	567	54	Hornby
■ LMS 'Crab' 2-6-0	180	17	Bachmann
■ BR 'Standard Five' 4-6-0	55	5.2	Bachmann
■ BR 'Standard Four' 4-6-0	30	2.8	Bachmann
■ LMS Ivatt '4MT' 2-6-0	55	5.2	Bachmann
■ LMS Ivatt '2MT' 2-6-0	80	7.6	Bachmann

Table 6 – Ready-to-run LMR mixed traffic tanks

Locomotive	Number	%	RTR
■ LMS Stanier '4MT' 2-6-4T	206	26	Hornby
■ LMS Fowler '4MT' 2-6-4T	116	14.5	Hornby
■ LMS/BR Fairburn '4MT' 2-6-4T	102	13	Bachmann
■ BR 'Standard Four' 2-6-4T	45	5.6	Bachmann
■ LMS/BR Ivatt '2MT' 2-6-2T	91	11	Bachmann

Table 7 – Ready-to-run LMR freight tender classes

Locomotive	Number	%	RTR
■ LMS Stanier '8F' 2-8-0	613	24.7	Hornby
■ 'WD' '8F' 2-8-0	263	10.6	Bachmann
■ LMS 'G2a' 0-8-0	185	7.5	Bachmann
■ MR/LMS '4F' 0-6-0	693	28	Hornby

variant which were fitted with condensing apparatus and markedly different in appearance. A further sub-class of 80 locomotives, numbered 6700 to 6779, were built without vacuum brake or Automatic Train Control equipment and confined to shunting – something for modellers to note.

It is worth mentioning one other freight tank, the '94XX', which reached a total of 201 and represented 14% of Western Region freight tanks. There is no current model, but Lima did produce one some years ago. The body was quite good, but the chassis was poor.

The Southern Region

The Southern, like the Western, was basically the pre-nationalisation company. In terms of locomotive distribution it was the region which proved the exception to the rule, having roughly equal numbers in each category – Table 11. In 1955 the 30 'Merchant Navy' 4-6-2s were all in original air-smoothed condition, which is not available as a ready-to-run model. The current model is only suitable for the year 1956 onwards.

The popular Bachmann model of the Maunsell 'Lord Nelson' 4-6-0 has not been in the current catalogues for a couple of years, but 2008 is different, as Bachmann is releasing a new number variation on this powerful locomotive: 30865 *Sir John Hawkins* in BR lined green.

The Maunsell 'Schools' 4-4-0 was one of Hornby's most popular models and a fully re-tooled locomotive drive model is due towards the end of 2008. The 'L1' 4-4-0 is an even older model, but it does turn up second hand. One further '3P' 4-4-0 was the LSWR Drummond 'T9'. There were 36 of the class left in 1955 making 12.9% of the SR fleet and a model is expected from Hornby soon.

Only two SR passenger tanks are available ready-to-run. The largest by far is the Drummond 'M7' 0-4-4T, whose 103 members make 46.4% of passenger tanks on the Southern. The only other class is the Stroudley 'Terrier' or 'A1X' 0-6-0T with 13 members and 5.9%. Both of these models are produced by Hornby.

The Southern mixed traffic classes – Table 12 – were quite numerous with both pre-grouping survivors and new BR Standards alongside Southern Railway built classes providing plenty of variety for the modeller. Five out of the 12 Southern Region mixed traffic classes are available ready-to-run making well over half the total of 383.

However, at this time, 1955, the 'Light Pacifics' – 66 'West Country' and 44 'Battle of Britain' 4-6-2s – were all in original air-smoothed condition. Rebuilding did not begin until 1957 and ceased in 1961 when a total of 60 had been completed. For a Southern Region layout set after 1959 you can have both original and rebuilt Bulleids and they can be used on freight as well. The mixed traffic designation was a hangover from the war, when passenger locomotive construction was restricted, but Bulleid even timetabled some freight workings to maintain the pretence. In practice freight was very rarely seen behind the Bulleid 'Pacifics', but they could certainly be found on parcels traffic

Table 8a – Ready-to-run WR passenger tender classes

Locomotive	Number	%	RTR
■ GWR 'King' 4-6-0	30	13.5	Hornby
■ GWR 'Castle' 4-6-0	167	75.2	Hornby

Table 8b – Ready-to-run WR passenger tanks

Locomotive	Number	%	RTR
■ GWR Collett '14XX' 0-4-2T	93	47.1	Hornby

Table 9 – Ready-to-run WR mixed traffic tender classes

Locomotive	Number	%	RTR
■ GWR 'Hall' 4-6-0	258	29.5	Bachmann
■ GWR 'Modified Hall' 4-6-0	71	8.1	Bachmann
■ GWR 'Grange' 4-6-0	76	8.7	Hornby
■ GWR 'Manor' 4-6-0	30	3.4	Bachmann
■ GWR '43XX' and '93XX' 2-6-0	211	24.1	Bachmann
■ GWR '2251' 0-6-0	120	13.7	Bachmann

Table 10 – Ready-to-run WR mixed traffic tanks

Locomotive	Number	%	RTR
■ GWR Collett '56XX' 0-6-2T	200	32.3	Bachmann
■ GWR '61XX' and '81XX' 2-6-2T	80	13	Hornby
■ GWR '5101' 2-6-2T	131	21.2	Hornby
■ GWR '45XX' and '4575' 2-6-2Ts	139	22.5	Bachmann

and on fast fitted goods such as the milk trains.

The mixed traffic tanks of the Southern Region provided a lot of variety for the modeller as they were branch line locomotives, equally at home on passenger as on goods – see Table 13.

On parts of the region the BR Standards replaced the very similar Fairburns and eventually the Fairburns were all sent back to the London Midland Region. The Ivatts were later replaced by the BR Standard versions, the 84000 2-6-2Ts, but instead of going back to the LMR they went to the Western section of the SR. The largest class of mixed traffic on the SR was the ex-LBSCR 'E4' 0-6-2T – 63 of these tanks made up 35.6% of all mixed traffic tanks, but sadly no ready-to-run model is available from the mass producers.

Southern freight traffic was not huge and loads were generally light. Not surprisingly, few models are available ready-to-run and only one freight tender locomotive is available: the Bulleid 'Q1' 0-6-0, from Hornby. Its 40 members constituted only 12.4% of the total.

There are currently no Southern freight tanks available, but two older, but now obsolete, models do appear on the tables. Both were small classes of just 10 members, being the ex-LBSCR 'E2' 0-6-0T once produced by Hornby and the ex-SECR Stirling 'R1' 0-6-0T which was made by Hornby Dublo and later Wrenn.

Eastern Region

We now come to the last three regions which are closely related, being part of the LNER. Like the LMS, the LNER lost its Scottish lines to the new Scottish Region, but its English lines were further divided into two new regions: the North Eastern and the Eastern.

The Eastern Region was formed of the southern lines of the LNER, basically the pre-grouping Great Eastern, Great Northern and Great Central Railways. The London and North Eastern Railway, despite being relatively poor, was lucky to have one of the greatest locomotive engineers of all time and the locomotive tables are full of his designs, none more so than the passenger classes – Table 14.

The Southern Region of BR had more passenger traffic to contend with than freight. Rebuilt 'Battle of Britain' 4-6-2 34052 *Lord Dowding* departs London Waterloo with the 6pm to Salisbury as BR 'Standard Four' 2-6-4T 80012 approaches with Empty Coaching Stock on 26 August 1966. Brian Stephenson.

The 'Pacifics' are well known, the 4-6-0s perhaps less well. The 'B17/6' is the 'Sandringham' or 'Footballer' class, one of Hornby's older tender drive models. The 'B12' was an even older model re-introduced as one of the first new models from China;

it was a faithful copy of the original right down to the tender fitted 'chuff-chuff' mechanism!

Passenger tanks were not numerous and none are available ready-to-run, so we have to rely on the mixed traffic tank engines to do

the honours. The mixed traffic classes of the LNER varied from the powerful 'K3' 2-6-0 and 'V2' 2-6-2 designed by Sir Nigel Gresley to the reliable and plentiful Thompson 'B1' 4-6-0, as outlined in Table 15. Bachmann provides the modeller with a range of mixed traffic tender locomotives, covering all the principal types and also obliges with the tank engines, including the Fairburn and BR 'Standard Four' classes – Table 16.

However, the number of tank engines available doesn't do justice to the full range in service. In fact the largest two classes are not available. The largest, at 134 members, is the GER 'N7' 0-6-2T, essential for any East Anglian modeller. There were also 90 of Thompson's 'L1' 2-6-4Ts.

Only two freight classes with LNER heritage have been turned into ready-to-run models (Table 17) and these are left to represent about one third of the 1,299 freight tender locomotives on the Eastern Region, but the largest class is sadly not represented. There were 266 of the Robinson 'O4' 2-8-0s – the First

Table 11 – Ready-to-run SR passenger tender classes

Locomotive	Number	%	RTR
■ Bulleid 'Merchant Navy' 4-6-2	30	10.7	Hornby
■ Maunsell 'Lord Nelson' 4-6-0	16	5.7	Bachmann
■ Maunsell 'King Arthur' 4-6-0	69	14.6	Hornby
■ Maunsell 'Schools' 4-4-0	40	14.2	Hornby
■ SECR/SR 'L1' 4-4-0	15	5.3	Hornby

Table 12 – Ready-to-run SR mixed traffic tender classes

Locomotive	Number	%	RTR
■ Bulleid 'Light Pacific' 4-6-2	110	28.7	Hornby
■ BR 'Standard Five' 4-6-0	25	6.5	Bachmann
■ SR Maunsell 'N' 2-6-0	80	20.9	Bachmann
■ BR 'Standard Four' 2-6-0	30	7.8	Bachmann
■ BR 'Standard Four' 4-6-0	13	3.4	Bachmann

Table 13 – Ready-to-run SR mixed traffic tanks

Locomotive	Number	%	RTR
■ LMS/BR Fairburn 2-6-4T	34	19.2	Bachmann
■ BR 'Standard Four' 2-6-4T	13	7.3	Bachmann
■ 2MT 2-6-2T LMR Ivatt	35	19.8	Bachmann

World War equivalent of the 'WD' 2-8-0. A model could appear on any livery from pre-grouping Great Central, though to BR and not forgetting the 100 acquired by the GWR from government surplus stock at the end of the First World War. These were condensed to 80 of which 50 were overhauled and continued to serve through the Second World War. In 1955, 20 of the GWR 'O4s', or 'Rods' as they were known, remained in service. To quote from the book 'Robinson Locomotives' "...they became more widespread than any other British class... ...the only areas where they were not seen at some time or another were the north of Scotland, mid-Wales and the Southern Railway".

In terms of tank engines, Table 18, again there is only a limited supply. The Lima model of the 'J50' 0-6-0T is not current, but the other two classes are quite reasonable models, the 'Austerity', or 'J94' to give it its full LNER classification, in particular. Hornby's 'J52' is one of their many tanks which sit on the standard 0-6-0 chassis.

Table 14 – Ready-to-run ER passenger tender classes

Locomotive	Number	%	RTR
■ Peppercorn 'A1' 4-6-2	22	8.2	Bachmann
■ Gresley 'A4' 4-6-2	19	7.1	Bachmann/Hornby
■ Gresley 'A3' 4-6-2	33	12.3	Hornby
■ Gresley 'B17/6' 4-6-0	42	15.7	Hornby
■ Holden 'B12' 4-6-0	42	15.7	Hornby

Table 15 – Ready-to-run ER mixed traffic tender classes

Locomotive	Number	%	RTR
■ Gresley 'K3' 2-6-0	120	18.6	Bachmann
■ Gresley 'V2' 2-6-2	76	11.8	Bachmann
■ Thompson 'B1' 4-6-0	259	40.1	Bachmann
■ LMS/BR Ivatt '4MT' 2-6-0	56	8.7	Bachmann

Table 16 – Ready-to-run ER mixed traffic tanks

Locomotive	Number	%	RTR
■ Fairburn 2-6-4T	28	5.9	Bachmann
■ BR 'Standard Four' 2-6-4T	22	4.6	Bachamnn
■ Gresley 'N2' 0-6-2T	91	19	Hornby

Table 17 – Ready-to-run ER freight tender classes

Locomotive	Number	%	RTR
■ Riddles 'WD' 2-8-0	255	19.6	Bachmann
■ Gresley 'J39' 0-6-0	169	13	Bachmann

Table 18 – Ready-to-run ER freight tanks classes

Locomotive	Number	%	RTR
■ Gresley 'J50' 0-6-0T	95	26.1	Lima
■ 'Austerity' ('J94') 0-6-0ST	23	6.3	Dapol/Hornby
■ Gresley 'J52' 0-6-0ST	65	17.9	Hornby

North-Eastern Region

In creating six regions out of the four grouped companies, some fragmenting of those companies was inevitable. At the time of the 1923 grouping, a Scottish company had been rejected only to be revived in 1948, but the North Eastern region was something of a surprise; being virtually a re-creation of the pre-grouping North Eastern Railway. It left the LNER split into three and the North Eastern Region was by far the smallest of the six.

The Hornby 'D49' 4-4-0, see Table 19, is one of their older models dating from the 'year of the 4-4-0' when the Southern 'Schools' was also introduced. The model was of a 'D49/1' and most of these were named after 'Shire' counties of the LNER, but were equipped with ex Great Central Railway tenders. Second-hand Hornby 'D49s' can quite easily be found, but it may be worth hoping for a new model given

that Hornby is introducing a new 4-4-0 chassis for the 'Schools' and 'T9' which share a common wheelbase.

There are no passenger tanks available ready-to-run for the NER, but more than half were of the 'A5' and 'A8' 4-6-2T classes, an unusual wheel arrangement for British tanks, and confined to the Eastern and North-Eastern regions. A ready-to-run model is unlikely so it will be necessary to turn to the mixed traffic tanks for secondary and branch passenger trains.

Bachmann offers a pretty comprehensive range of mixed traffic tender locomotives for the NER, Table 20, and the same can be said for mixed traffic tank engines, Table 21, where the same company produces four classes. The latter two classes, 'V1' and 'V3', were outwardly the same, just having different pressure boilers and a choice of bunkers. Bachmann have produced

both classes. The modeller of the North Eastern Region has been well served with mixed traffic classes, but none are native designs of the North Eastern Railway, a lack which is noticeable when considering the freight locomotives, as shown in Table 22.

Sadly no models of the numerous pre-grouping NER freight tender classes are available despite their heavy workload. At the grouping in 1923 the North Eastern Railway was the largest carrier of coal and had a fleet of locomotives which were still active in 1955. Foremost of these was the Raven 'Q6' 0-8-0 of which the full class of 120 were still in service. There were also over 200 0-6-0s of Worsdell classes 'J25', 'J26' and 'J27'. The total of 565 freight tender locomotives exceeded all other categories of North Eastern Region locomotives, only the mixed traffic tender type, at 394, comes

Table 19 – Ready-to-run NER passenger tender classes

Locomotive	Number	%	RTR
■ Peppercorn 'A1' 4-6-2	22	18	Bachmann
■ Gresley 'A4' 4-6-2	8	6.5	Hornby/Bachmann
■ Gresley 'A3' 4-6-2	26	21.2	Hornby
■ Gresley 'D49' 4-4-0	53	43	Hornby

Table 20 – Ready-to-run NER mixed traffic tender classes

Locomotive	Number	%	RTR
■ Gresley 'K3' 2-6-0	41	10.4	Bachmann
■ Gresley 'V2' 2-6-2	65	16.5	Bachmann
■ Thompson 'B1' 4-6-0	80	20.3	Bachmann
■ LMS/BR Ivatt '4MT' 2-6-0	41	10.4	Bachmann

Table 21 – Ready-to-run NER mixed traffic tanks classes

Locomotive	Number	%	RTR
■ LMS/BR Fairburn 2-6-4T	7	10.5	Bachmann
■ BR 'Standard Four' 2-6-4T	5	7.5	Bachmann
■ Gresley 'V3' 2-6-2T	17	25.2	Bachmann
■ Gresley 'V1' 2-6-2T	15	22	Bachmann

Table 22 – Ready-to-run NER freight tender classes

Locomotive	Number	%	RTR
■ Riddles 'WD' 2-8-0	109	19.3	Bachmann
■ Gresley 'J39' 0-6-0	94	16.6	Bachmann

Table 23 – Ready-to-run NER freight tanks classes

Locomotive	Number	%	RTR
■ 'J94' 0-6-0ST	45	17	Hornby/Dapol
■ NER/BR Worsdell 'J72' 0-6-0T	97	36.6	Bachmann

close to this total. Clearly the NER was a region with substantial freight traffic.

With this volume of freight there was a need for tank engines to marshall and work trip freight, as shown in Table 23. The Ministry of Supply 'Austerity' 0-6-0ST was built in large numbers and found use in many collieries, something which recent Hornby models have shown. The LNER bought 75 of these useful locomotives in 1946 and classified them 'J94'.

The 'J72' class has the unique distinction of being built over a period of 53 years from the first in 1898 through further batches under Raven, then by the LNER after grouping and finally a batch of 28 ordered by Peppercorn as North Eastern Region CME and built in 1949-51.

Scottish Region

We now come to the last of the six regions, furthest north and in many ways the most interesting, given that the locomotive stock consisted of pre-grouping Scottish designs, ex-LMS and ex-LNER and two post-nationalisation classes specific to Scotland, the 'WD' 2-10-0s and the BR 'Clan' 4-6-2. To the modeller who wants plenty of locomotive variety, a well chosen Scottish prototype can provide all that might be required.

Most of the passenger classes listed in Table 24 have already been mentioned in other regions listings. All other passenger classes, both tender and tank, were pre-grouping designs, and no ready-to-run models are available, as usual mixed traffic classes provide any further passenger motive power which may be required, as listed in Table 25. There were a further 13 mixed traffic tender classes totalling 91 locomotives and these include some ready-to-run models such as the ex-LMS Ivatt '4MT' 2-6-0, Ivatt '2MT' 2-

6-0 and the BR 'Standard Four' 2-6-0, all produced as by Bachmann.

The spread of the later LMS designs of Fairburn and Ivatt to other regions was something which made them in effect forerunners of the BR Standard classes. In several cases they were copied almost exactly – the Ivatt '2MT' 2-6-0s and 2-6-2Ts in particular. Table 26 lists the mixed traffic tank locomotives currently available ready-to-run for the Scottish Region.

There are sadly few freight locomotives available to the modeller of the Scottish Region. The ubiquitous Riddles 'WD' 2-8-0 appears on the freight tender tables with 59 members and covering just 8.1% of the fleet. The only other significant class is the LMS '4F' 0-6-0 which manages a meagre 49 examples out of the total 731 freight tender locomotives on the Scottish Region. The LNER 'J39' class had just 26 members on the Scottish Region, but the Stanier '8F' is the smallest ready-to-run class available with just eight on the region, five inherited from the LMS and three from the LNER, all other classes are pre-grouping Scottish types and have not attracted the attention of the ready-to-run manufacturers.

The same is true of the freight tanks. Of a total of 305 locomotives, 138 were Caledonian McIntosh '3F' 0-6-0Ts, leaving the remaining 167 locomotive shared between 14 classes, seven of which were dock tanks of various kinds. Four of the remaining classes are available as ready-to-run models. Table 27 lists them in descending order.

This concludes our look at the locomotive stock of the six regions of British Railways in 1955. But why 1955? The years 1955 to 1957 had always seemed to be the classic period of post-war BR steam. The long years of austerity were finally ending and the vast majority of the population took their holidays in Britain, but huge changes were just around the corner.

The most important transport announcement of 1955 was the

In 1955 there were only 70 of the eventual 251 BR '9F' 2-10-0s in traffic, as construction continued. The class were tasked with the heaviest of freight trains, but on occasion, even though they were freight locomotives, they appeared at the head of express trains on the Western Region. On the Eastern Region, the East Coast Main Line at Sandy, BR '9F' 92183 heads an up freight on 28 May 1961. M Fox/Rail Archive Stephenson.

publication of BR's Modernisation Plan which sought to address some of these problems. Amongst its main provision was replacement of many steam locomotives by diesel and electric traction, along with extension of electrification and other improvements to the railway network. The Modernisation Plan recognised the need to replace steam, but no one envisaged the time span being as little as 12 years.

Production of the new Standard steam locomotives was in full swing and would continue for another five years until BR '9F' 92220 *Evening Star*, the last steam locomotive to be built for British Railways, was named on 18 March 1960, but even then, few people would have thought its working life would only last five years. If you should choose 1955 as a year to model, it offers great potential and now you can understand how the balance of power was split between express passenger, mixed traffic and freight locomotives too.

Table 24 – Ready-to-run ScR passenger tender classes

Locomotive	Number	%	RTR
■ LNER Gresley 'A3' 4-6-2	19	6	Hornby
■ LMS Stanier 'Jubilee' 4-6-0	29	9.1	Bachmann
■ LNER Gresley 'D49' 4-4-0	22	7	Hornby
■ LMS Fowler '2P' 4-4-0	74	23	Hornby

Table 25 – Ready-to-run ScR mixed traffic tender classes

Locomotive	Number	%	RTR
■ LNER Gresley 'K3' 2-6-0	31	5.2	Bachmann
■ LNER Gresley 'V2' 2-6-2	43	7.2	Bachmann
■ LMS Stanier 'Black Five' 4-6-0	262	43.6	Hornby
■ LNER Thompson 'B1' 4-6-0	70	11.6	Bachmann
■ BR 'Standard Five' 4-6-0	39	6.5	Bachmann
■ LMS Hughes/Fowler 'Crab' 2-6-0	65	10.8	Bachmann

Table 26 – Ready-to-run ScR mixed traffic tank classes

Locomotive	Number	%	RTR
■ LMS/BR Fairburn 2-6-4T	106	31	Bachmann
■ BR 'Standard Four' 2-6-4T	46	13.5	Bachmann
■ LNER Gresley 'V1' 2-6-2T	48	14	Bachmann

Table 27 – Ready-to-run ScR freight tank classes

Locomotive	Number	–	RTR
■ Ex-NER 'J83' 0-6-0T	39		Hornby
■ Ex-NER/LNER 'J72' 0-6-0T	12		Bachmann
■ LNER 'J50' 0-6-0T	7		Lima (obsolete)

Ashington

Third-rail Electric Multiple Units aren't always the first choice for layout builders because there are no ready-to-run models. But that didn't stop Dave Kent pressing ahead to build Ashington, which has now attended more than 40 model railway exhibitions! *Photography, Chris Nevard.*

The Southern Region of BR was a unique place primarily because of the large number of Electric Multiple Units (EMUs) which were employed on commuter trains serving the giant commuter belt to the south of London. They operated from a third rail which carried a 750v DC current, which wasn't entirely unique, but the frequency of services certainly was.

For some it bore no interest whatsoever – steam traction was, for many reasons, far more attractive to enthusiasts, but the EMUs had their own charm rattling through complex junctions filled to the rafters with businessmen making their daily journeys to and from the capital.

For Dave Kent, the Southern Region's EMUs provided the inspiration for his 'OO' gauge layout and now, seven years after Ashington attended its first show, the layout has attended more than 40 events with further appearances in the pipeline.

Hornby Magazine featured Ashington in its fifth issue and in the first annual Layout of the Year competition, with the winner voted for by the readers, Ashington came joint fourth with Enginewood – see pages 92-99 for more on Enginewood.

The biggest problem with modelling the Southern Region's EMUs is the lack of ready-to-run models – there are none at present, although Bachmann is working on a 'OO' gauge model of the 4-CEP, a First Generation BR designed express unit formed of four vehicles. Instead, anyone modelling this area of the country and wanting multiple units has to turn to kit manufacturers.

But what prompted Dave to model the BR Southern Region EMUs? "Ian Kirk's kits were the catalyst for Ashington when he produced a plastic kit for the 2-BIL EMU. I am happy with plastic kits, having built the majority of the Airfix aircraft range when Woolworth's used to sell them from 2 shillings (10p) each, and at the time Branchlines of Exeter was providing a 2-BIL package which included motor, wheels, detailing kit and full instructions on improving it," Dave said.

"I must confess, at the time I did not have the knowledge of what components were available, no computer or Internet, so the Branchlines package was an offer not to be missed."

The Kirk 2-BIL formed a learning curve as far as construction was concerned because, although Dave was familiar with plastic kits, the detailing pack included white metal and brass components, materials which he had yet to work with. "The detailing took longer than the basic kit construction," commented Dave, but the end result I feel was worth the time."

The Southern Region's EMUs went through several phases of development. A Southern Railway-designed 2-HAL, 2656, stands next to a BR- designed 2-HAP unit at the stabling point.

Multiple line-up: From left stands a 4-BEP, a 2-HAL, a MLV, a 3D DEMU and a 2-HAP. All these units have been built from kits for Ashington.

Success with the 2-BIL lead to a further order for a Phoenix 2-HAL kit, from Branchlines again, although they are now only available from the Southern Railways Group (www.srgroup.fsnet.co.uk) and this produced another new material and new problems to overcome as it featured an aluminium shell with white metal ends and fittings. One of the big problems came in the roof area. The older Southern Region EMUs featured wiring conduits along the roof, but the question was how to stick brass or plastic to aluminium? Soldering was deemed out of the question and Superglues were still in their infancy when working on the 2-HAL. Persistence paid off and Dave found his method and added a second unit to the fledgling fleet.

Where next? As a newcomer to SR EMU modelling, research and discoveries became an important part of the fleets, development and the next manufacturer Dave became aware of was Southern Pride. These kits include pre-printed plastic bodyside overlays on a clear plastic side with white metal castings for the

Ashington stock list

Class	Number	Manufacturer	Notes
Hampshire 3-H DEMU[1]	1109	DC Kits	Tenshendo motor plus added detail
Oxted 3-D DEMU[1]	1304	DC kits	Tenshendo motor plus added detail
2-BIL EMU[2]	2047	Ian Kirk	Dummy unit with Branchlines detail kit
2-BIL EMU[3]	2134	Ian Kirk	Black Beetle motor with Branchlines detail kit
2-HAL EMU[4]	2656	Phoenix	Branchlines motor and detailing kit
2-HAP EMU[5]	5634	No Nonsense Kit	Black Beetle motor
2-EPB EMU[6]	5723	Southern Pride	Southern Pride motor
4-BEP EMU[7]	7016	Southern Pride	Tenshendo motor
MLV[8]	68004	Southern Pride	Tenshendo motor

Notes:
1. 3-H and 3-D: Three-car diesel electric multiple units introduced 1957 and 1962 respectively
2. 2-BIL: Two-car suburban electric multiple unit introduced in 1936
3. 2-BIL: Two-car suburban electric multiple unit introduced in 1938
4. 2-HAL: Two-car suburban electric multiple unit introduced in 1939
5. 2-HAP: Two-car suburban electric multiple unit introduced in 1957
6. 2-EPB: Two-car suburban electric multiple unit introduced in 1955
7. 4-BEP: Four-car electric multiple unit with buffet car introduced in 1956
8. MLV: Single-car electric motorised luggage van introduced in 1959

cab fronts of each unit. Dave's first purchase from Southern Pride was a single vehicle Motor Luggage Van (MLV) quickly followed by a BR built 2-EPB suburban unit. Commenting on the kits, Dave said: "These kits go together rather quickly and it is only your preference for painting and detailing which prolongs the build time."

As the fleet grew, so did the desire to have a layout to run them on. The ambition was to create a portable layout to display the fleet on and, as a member of the Worthing Model Railway Club, Dave struck a deal where he financed the layout and club members assisted with the electrics. In return the newly created Ashington could be exhibited as a club layout too. Good for everyone!

Building Ashington

Dave takes up the story: "The name Ashington comes from a small village just north of Worthing on the A24. Ideas were put forward in the early years of railway building for a line to run north from Worthing and the route would have probably been along what is now the A24. A connection between the Steyning branch and Pulborough was also planned and could have passed by the village. I am frequently reminded at exhibitions of the Ashington in Northumberland!

"The layout is made up of three baseboards 4ft x 2ft, which gives a total 12ft length. Construction is simply 2in x 1in timber framework screwed and glued with 1ft between cross members to form a rigid structure. Integral legs are 2in x 2in timber and the tops are made from Sundeala board. Once the baseboards were constructed they were painted with a dilute PVA solution to seal the wood and particularly the Sundeala tops to eliminate the risk of warping. The location of the cross-members and legs (when folded for storage) were marked on the top of the boards so that they could be taken into consideration when the track plan was drawn on top: after all, I didn't want a cross-member in the way of a point motor.

"To show off a collection of locomotives, an engine shed or Motive Power Depot (MPD) would be appropriate. With EMUs I decided a stabling point and carriage shed would be ideal. I made a trip to West Worthing and Littlehampton sheds to gather information and a track plan began to formulate. It was essential that the track plan allowed for an element of play, but at the same time was plausible to the viewing public if at an exhibition.

"Fiddle yards are not prototypical, but are accepted as part of a layout, particularly one on the exhibition circuit as they introduce an element of surprise and somewhere for the trains to 'go'. The fiddle yard on Ashington has two exits – one through the station and one through to the stabling point/carriage shed. To add operator interest, a line was taken out of the side of the carriage shed with the intention that the rear of the carriage shed would also be a fiddle yard. I did not like the way this turned out so the fiddle yard became a main line and in time meant I had to add scenery as well.

"At one of the earlier exhibitions it was pointed out to me that the shed roads should be numbered 3, 2, 1 not 1, 2, 3. Apparently the

Two designs of Diesel Electric Multiple Unit (DEMU) stand side-by-side in the stabling sidings. On the left is a 3D Oxted unit and nearest the camera is a 3H Hampshire unit.

Metcalfe card building kits form the basis of the street scene on Ashington.

In a classic early BR scene, the 2-BIL which started Dave Kent on the road to building Ashington runs through the station as a 2-HAL unit leaves the stabling point and disappears under the road bridge in the background.

numbering starts from the main line. Of course when the shed was constructed, the mainline was a fiddle yard!

"With baseboard construction completed, they were transported down to the club for track laying and wiring up. I've used Peco Code 75 track with code 60 rail for the 'electrified' third rail. Track laid and wired up, I moved the layout back home for the scenic work to begin. The first task was to paint the sides of the rails with a rust colour before

laying 'N' gauge ballast. Ballasting was actually done over a period of six weeks (to maintain sanity) in between other scenic work.

"Next was installation and painting of the third rail (it gets in the way of painting the main rail sides and ballasting if you install it before). The insulators produced by Peco are of a flexible material and the technique is to drill a hole in the end of the sleeper, thread the insulators onto the third rail and push into the pre-drilled holes. If you do not push

straight down into the hole, the insulators have a habit of bending and then disappearing into orbit or the carpet to be lost forever. An added feature installed after all the ballasting had been completed was an Express Models 'blue flash' to represent the arcing that occurs with electric units between the pick up shoe and the third rail."

Southern fortune

Another prominent feature of the BR Southern Region, after the EMUs, is concrete – and lots of it! After the Second World War the Southern Railway, and later BR's Southern Region, replaced some station buildings with elaborate concrete structures, but equally platform edging, footbridges and fencing were also made from concrete.

Southern Region modellers are fortunate that many of these structures, save station buildings, are available in kit form including a typical SR footbridge, fencing and platform edging – the main ingredients. The platform and overbridge for

A 'blue flash' has been installed next to one of the baseboard joins to represent the arching which occurs between the pick-up shoe of units and the third-rail.

Ashington were made from Wills plastic sheets and kits and Peco platform edging. However, the signalbox is a mixture of a Wills and Ratio kit with a fully-detailed interior, modified externally with a walkway along the windows.

As well as making good use of readily available plastic kits, Metcalfe card building kits have been used to create parts of the layout too. "Metcalfe buildings make up the high street and to disguise the exposed cardboard edges, I purchased a cheap set of felt tip pens and chose an appropriate colour to run down the corner of the buildings. I recommend checking the colour of the pen on a piece of paper first because the shade of the felt is not necessarily the same colour as on the ink," Dave added.

He continued: "The main structure on the layout is the carriage shed, some 40in in length. I used modellers' licence to give a representation of the shed, basing it on photographs I took of carriage sheds at West Worthing and Littlehampton. On the original an inspection gantry ran the length on both sides of the roof, but has long since disappeared from the West Worthing example.

"The main walls are made from a type of ABS which started life as a notice board (railway modellers are no strangers to recycling) and overlaid with Wills sheeting. The roof is removable for track cleaning and is made from a framework of plastic covered with Wills clear panels and individual asbestos sheets cut from Slaters corrugated plastic sheet.

"To create the backscene I used 3mm plywood, which was first painted with white emulsion left over from a DIY project. A test pot of a suitable blue colour was obtained and with a brush of blue paint in one hand and white in the other I proceeded to paint the sky. The joy of emulsion is that it dries relatively quickly and if you do not like the result you can paint over it and try again. The printed back scenes which form the lower sections are a mixture of Peco and Townscene

sheets available from Freestone Model Accessories. I have cut the sheets up, changed the roofline and mounted some buildings on thick card. This has ¼in blocks stuck to the rear, which produces a relief effect against the other buildings."

First exhibition
As with any layout, Ashington has developed over time. By his own admission, Ashington's first exhibition appearance offered a more basic layout compared to what there is now. A Wrenn Brighton Belle Pullman EMU was used for a while to fill up the sidings, but as the fleet developed there was less need to keep this unit in the fleet.

One diversion from the EMU fleet is a steam hauled push-pull set, a London, Brighton and South Coast

Railway (LBSCR) type produced from Roxey kits, which was originally hauled by a Bachmann Ivatt '2MT' 2-6-2T on the layout. However, with the introduction of Hornby's superb model of the Drummond 'M7' 0-4-4T – a common performer on push-pull sets on the Southern Region, Dave added one to the roster together with a new push-pull set of Maunsell design built from Colin Ashby coaches with a Branchlines detailing and brass overlay kit. Dave added: "This is purely for variety on the layout, but I like it."

When built, two-car operation was envisaged, but again new releases from kit manufacturers mean that Dave has changed his ideals. "DC kits started producing Southern Region diesel-electric

The signalbox is a modified kit with full interior detail. A Southern Railway designed 2-HAL passes the 'box before pausing in the station to collect passengers.

The 4-BEP corridor unit enters the carriage sidings from the fiddle yard. At four vehicles long, this is the largest unit in the fleet.

The carriage shed is almost 40in long and can almost accommodate a full four-car EMU. The two stabling roads alongside have a typical raised concrete walkway between adding further to the depot feel. On the left a 3H Diesel Electric Multiple Units stands alongside a 2-HAL.

multiple units (DEMUs) so a Hampshire and an Oxted three-car unit have since joined the fleet along with a 4-BEP four-car unit from Southern Pride.

"With the majority of the EMU kits I have built, it was a case of adding detail to improve the model. One manufacturer however does produce kits to a very high standard and no additional or very little detailing is required. That is No Nonsense Kits (no connection, just a satisfied customer!) and the 2-HAP I built was a pleasure, if somewhat stressful because I didn't want to mess the kit up! It is nearly all brass and the bends in the bodywork have been rolled for you. You could tell the quality of the kit by the way that the components were packed.

"A lot of EMU kits are now available in kit form, but Bachmann's 4-CEP is eagerly awaited. Manufacturers have kept away from EMUs, probably due to lack of sales, but Hornby produce a Class 466 Networker. I have one in my collection although it is too modern for Ashington."

"Arguments still rage about the lack of ready-to-run SR EMUs, but as Bachmann Managing Director

Graham Hubbard said in a recent article discussing the forthcoming 4-CEP model: "If it 'bombs' that will be the end of the argument." That's a message for all Southern fans and third rail enthusiasts in particular: support the manufacturers or it is back to building kits!"

"I hope Ashington proves inspirational and that if you are truly interested in third-rail, you will not be put off modelling a layout because

of the lack of ready-to-run models. I am not 100% happy with any of the models I have built, but I am getting better.

■ My thanks to my regular exhibition operators (they know who they are), those exhibition managers who have invited Ashington to their shows and Chris Nevard for the excellent photographs.

In the station 2-HAP 5634 is ready to depart as a 2-BIL leaves after terminating at Ashington.

Ashington stats

Owner:	Dave Kent
Builder:	Dave Kent and Worthing MRC
Scale:	'OO'
Track:	Peco Code 75 with Code 60 rail on Peco insulators for third rail
Length:	12ft
Width:	2ft
Layout type:	Fiddle yard-station/carriage shed
Period/Region:	1950s/60s Southern EMUs

Ashington Track Diagram
Each square represents 1 square foot. Not to scale

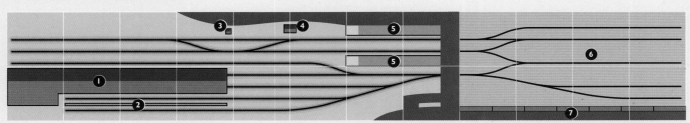

Key

1	Carriage shed	4	Signalbox
2	Stabling point	5	Platforms
3	Permanent way hut	6	Fiddle yard
		7	Low relief buildings

Digital Command Control: a beginner's guide

Digital Command Control is advancing rapidly and is gaining more popularity, but there are many questions that surround the system. MIKE WILD and IAN MORTON explores the world of DCC to provide a beginners guide.

What is Digital Command Control, also known as 'DCC'? There are many myths about it, but with the likes of Bachmann and Hornby now producing complete DCC train sets this control system is becoming more popular, particularly with new modellers who are starting afresh in the hobby today.

Until recently, almost every layout was based around a controller that provided power to the track which increased the speed of the train when the control knob was turned – Direct Control (DC). It was simple, but allowed only one locomotive to be controlled at a time per controller. As soon as you started building up a fleet of locomotives, life got more complicated, as with conventional systems isolating sections are required to 'park' a locomotive when it is not in use. In some cases this can be achieved by changing the direction of the points, but in other applications, such as locomotive yards, isolating sections with switches are needed. Of course isolating sections means wiring, and this can prove to be a real headache to the uninitiated.

With DCC those looms of 'spaghetti-like' wiring strung beneath the baseboards can be a thing of the past, in fact, unless you are building a portable layout with sectional boards, the only wires you *have* to install for DCC operation are those from the controller to the track – that's it! Of course, it isn't always so clear cut, as complex track work will require additional electrical feeds – as with DC control – and if you want electric point motors and other gadgets on your layout, then more wiring will be needed, but not everybody has these featureson their model railways.

Illustrating the simplicity of DCC are the recently-introduced Hornby Digital train sets. With these it is possible to open the box and have trains running with digital control in 15 minutes – if you don't want to pin down the track or build a complex layout based around the train set! All you have to do, even when there are points included, is set up the track, connect the DCC controller and away you go!

This is the simple side of DCC, but there are complex electronics inside the controller although you don't need to know anything about them – in the same way that you don't need

Opposite page: **Digital Command Control has revolutionised model railway operation. Without DCC this photograph wouldn't have been possible as the locomotives, all 'OO' gauge ready-to-run examples, are stationary with their lights turned on using a DCC controller. Two Hornby Class 50s, a Bachmann 37 and a Heljan 47 line-up on Dudley Road, Peter Harvey's atmospheric and compact diesel shed layout.** Chris Nevard.

A selection of Digital controllers. From left: Gaugemaster's Prodigy, Hornby's Select, Lenz's LH100 and Bachmann's Dynamis. Mike Wild.

The red tail lights of the Class 31 reflect in the bodyside of the Class 56 (both Hornby models) at Dudley Road. Both locomotives are being controlled independently by a Digital controller at the same time on Peter Harvey's layout.
Chris Nevard.

to know how an internal combustion engine works to drive a car. But what about other parts of DCC, like decoders – and why do you need them to run trains, what are functions, how do you run double-headed trains and what about all those terms that are appearing on the boxes of ready-to-run models like DCC ready and DCC on board?

What does DCC do?

DCC is helping to put the fun back into railway modelling and simplify operations. Digital control also allows more realistic operation of a model railway, as the real railway doesn't have large banks of switches to 'isolate' locomotives and neither does DCC. In these days of computer technology, endless television, and games consoles, model manufacturers are hard pressed to compete, but digital technology is slowly but surely winning a new audience for model railways.

In the same way as conventional controllers, DCC controllers have a control knob that increases and decreases train speed, but in addition there is a keypad – generally with numbers 0-9 – and several other buttons. These buttons and keys are all used in the control of trains. Each locomotive used on a digital railway has to be given an 'address' so that the technology inside the decoder and controller can recognise which locomotive (or train) you want to control.

DCC systems can then control several locomotives independently on the same section of track without the need for section switches, isolating breaks or those troublesome wiring looms. Instead using the keypad to select which locomotive you control, you can set one train going, then at the touch of a button (literally) another train can follow it round on the same track at a different speed – or indeed, if you want, in the opposite direction

without affecting the progress of the first train that was set in motion. Its clever stuff, but you have to have your wits about you once more than one train is moving.

There is far more to DCC than just controlling the trains though, as the programmable nature of the equipment allows each user to change acceleration and deceleration characteristics for individual locomotives, control additional functions and other layout features. Double-heading is also simple with DCC. Rather than having to worry that two locomotives have identically paced motors, a DCC controller can do this for you.

As well as controlling the trains, DCC systems allow operators to control other functions on both the locomotives and off track accessories like point motors. On locomotives lighting can be controlled using what is commonly known as a 'function' key and similarly DCC locomotives with sound, which are, becoming

Wiring for analogue and digital

DCC can make building a model railway simpler, particularly when it comes to electrics. With DCC there is no need to install switches to 'park' locomotives as the controller and decoder chip do the work for you. These two diagrams illustrate how a simple layout can be wired for use of conventional analogue controllers (diagram 1) and how much simpler it can be with DCC (Diagram 2).

The top diagram requires three switches to afford a minimum level of flexibility whilst the DCC system does the same job, but without the need to install switches. In addition DCC controllers can also operate lights on locomotives and additional accessories such as points.

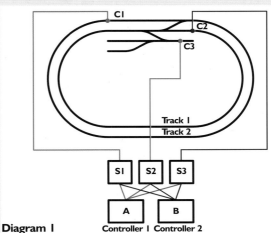

Diagram 1

S1- S3 Switches that allow the two controllers (A & B) to swap tracks or isolate sidings

C1-C3 Electrical connections from switches S1-S3/controllers

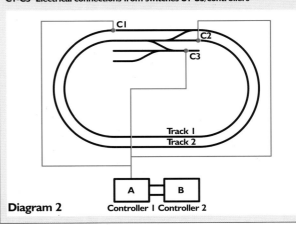

Diagram 2

increasingly popular can also be controlled through the 'function' key.

What about decoders?

Decoders are the microchips that have to be installed in locomotives not already fitted for digital operation. They are small, usually black, and the standard version have eight pins on the connecting base. The actual chip is rather like a small computer chip. Many new locomotive models now come with a decoder socket installed as standard, and, reflecting the layout of the chip plug, the socket has eight pin holes. The decoder has to be installed the right way round or it won't work.

Mention of chip installation brings up another important point about DCC models. Not all new models have DCC sockets as standard. Models that predate the influx of DCC systems will also be devoid of a decoder socket, and in some cases it can be a little tricky to install the decoder socket as well as the chip. On the other hand, Bachmann has also introduced a 21-pin chip for its most recent DCC sound fitted locomotives.

When buying a new ready-to-run model it is important to check what it says on the box. Some items won't mention DCC at all, where as others will say DCC ready, DCC sound or DCC on-board (see panel for explanation of DCC terms). Today's new models are highly detailed and, at the same time, they can be quite difficult to open for the installation of a decoder chip. For a new modeller the best option is to look for models marked DCC on-board, although

those with a little patience can install there own choice of decoder in a DCC ready model, but it's not always for the faint hearted.

Basic DCC systems

If you are contemplating DCC control for your layout it is important to choose the right system. There are many different systems available on the market, although fortunately most are designed around the same standards set by the National Model Railway Association in America. This means that whichever decoder you chose to equip your locomotives with, it will still operate with any system, so long as it states either in the description or instructions that the equipment is NMRA compliant.

The complexity of systems available varies greatly from the Hornby starter Select system to the impressive ESU Command Station which features an LCD display, two controllers and a vast numbers of functions. The main manufacturers of DCC equipment are Bachmann, Digitrax, Gaugemaster, Hornby, Lenz and ESU. These systems vary greatly in the way they are designed, but all are compliant with the NMRA DCC standards. Choosing the right control package is very much a personal process.

Digital versus analogue

Doubtless, if you haven't already plumped for Digital Command Control (DCC), you will have read about it and its capabilities. But DCC isn't the only option for controlling our trains, as DC, sometimes called conventional or analogue control, is

still very much in existence and is a good choice for many. But what's the difference, and how do you choose which type of control is right for you?

Model locomotives are, on the whole, powered by electricity fed through the rails. A controller connected to the rails controls the electricity fed into the rails. By varying the voltage and polarity of the electricity we can change the speed and direction of the locomotive. This is DC control and it has been around

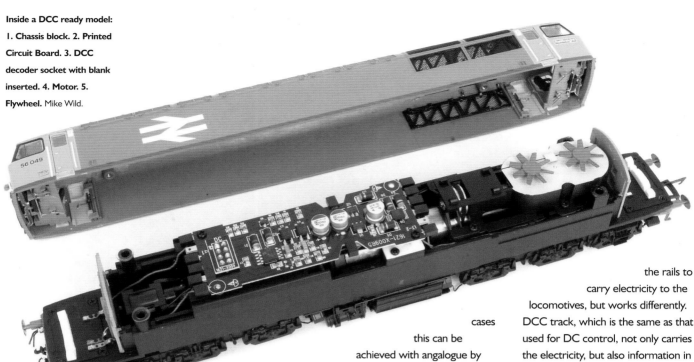

Inside a DCC ready model:
1. Chassis block. 2. Printed
Circuit Board. 3. DCC
decoder socket with blank
inserted. 4. Motor. 5.
Flywheel. Mike Wild.

since the very
first Hornby Dublo train
sets of the late-1930s.

If we want to have more than one
locomotive running at any time and
two tracks or more additional
controllers will be needed. If we have
more than one locomotive on the
layout to run on the same track, we
will need somewhere to isolate it
such as a siding or loop. In some

cases
this can be
achieved with angalogue by
simply changing a set of points to
isolate the locomotive from the
power supply, but in other cases we
will need to add switches and
insulated rail-joiners to isolate the
locomotives that are not being used
and connect the different controllers
to the locomotives that are.

Digital Control – the new order
DCC, which is an abbreviation of
Digital Command Control, still uses

the rails to
carry electricity to the
locomotives, but works differently.
DCC track, which is the same as that
used for DC control, not only carries
the electricity, but also information in
the form of electrical signals, which
are used to control the locomotives.

Each locomotive is fitted with an
electronic circuit called a decoder
that reads the signals sent by the
controller and responds accordingly.
The DCC controller supplies the
power and creates the signals used to
control the locomotives. With DCC
you do not need to isolate spare
locomotives and you can, depending
on your layout and reactions, run

Sometimes even a simple
layout will require section
switches to operate with
an analogue controller, but
with DCC switches can be
eliminated. Ian Morton.

Deciphering the code...

All new models have one of the following statements on the box. This is what they mean:

■ **No mention of DCC** – this means that the locomotive is a standard model without a decoder socket already installed. These can still be converted to DCC but require the owner to install a decoder socket and chip by removal of the body and use of a soldering iron to connect the wires to the motor. These locomotives can only be used with conventional control systems unless modified by the owner.

■ **DCC ready** – if the box has 'DCC ready' written on it, it means that the model is already equipped with a decoder socket, but no decoder. The owner can fit their own preference of decoder after purchase by removing the body. DCC ready locomotives can be used on conventional model railways without any alterations at all, but installation of a decoder is necessary for DCC operation.

To use a DCC ready locomotive with digital control is a simple case of plugging in a chip and the model will be ready to go.

■ **DCC Sound** – So far Bachmann is the only ready-to-run locomotive manufacturer for the UK market that has released a DCC Sound locomotive in 'OO' gauge. The term DCC Sound means that the model is fitted with a DCC Sound decoder and speaker system allowing its use on DCC systems. However, a DCC Sound locomotive cannot be used on a conventional layout.

■ **DCC On-board** – For new modellers looking to start out and stay with DCC operation this is the best logo to look out for, as it means the model is already equipped with a DCC decoder chip ready to be programmed into your system. Like the DCC Sound locomotives, DCC On-board models are designed to run on digitally controlled layouts only.

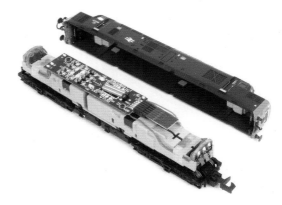

Although 'N' gauge models are now being fitted with tabs to solder a 6-pin decoder to, space is still at a premium inside – a necessary evil of adding enough weight to allow adequate haulage capacity. Mike Wild.

starting afresh than if you have a large collection of DC locomotives that will need to be converted, particularly if they pre-date the introduction of DCC ready locomotives.

Apart from the locomotives there is also the matter of points and accessories to consider. Point motors and other powered accessories can be operated conventionally using switches on the control panel, or from a DCC controller using special decoders. It is perfectly possible to use DCC for locomotives and conventional control for the accessories, or even vice-versa. If you opt for DCC control for point motors then you need to purchase special decoders which are mounted

more than one locomotive using a single controller.

There are many things to think about when deciding which system is best for you, and these will vary depending on your particular situation. For example it is a lot easier to choose DCC if you are

DCC controllers come with comprehensive manuals explaining their functions and how to operate them. It is worth keeping the manual to hand while familiarising yourself with the system. Mike Wild.

This is a Lenz LE1000E decoder chip. On the left is the decoder chip which communicates with the controller, while at the other end of the wires is the plug which connects to a standard 8-pin decoder socket. Mike Wild.

The direct chip from ZTC is a compact piece of equipment, more so than standard DCC chips which employ a series of wires to connect the chip to the plug. Mike Wild.

under the baseboard, these are then connected to the DCC controller and the accessories, such as point motors, being controlled.

The advantage of DCC control of accessories is that it can be done from a DCC controller, which is very convenient if you have a handheld controller and follow your train around the layout, or from a computer. If you use a computer, it can be set up so the computer displays a diagram of the layout and clicking the mouse on points changes them. Apart from saving the effort and expense of building a physical control panel it is also easy to modify the display if your layout changes or to add automation to certain areas, such as the fiddle yard or a branch line. However, you will need a computer to hand too!

The downside of DCC control of accessories is that if you don't use a computer it is impossible to stop two operators setting up conflicting routes, and the decoders are relatively expensive, typically costing £6 per point motor controlled.

Pros and cons – DC

With DC control any model with a motor can be powered without modification. You don't need to find extra space for a decoder, which is particularly relevant for scales such as 'N' and 'OO9' where space inside locomotive bodies is at a premium. But even small 'OO' and 'O' gauge locomotives can be short on space.

Just about any ready-to-run or kit-built locomotive that you will encounter can be run without any modification using a DC controller and 12v DC operation has been standard for many years and it is easier to understand and fault find than DCC. When things don't work it is usually a simple task to establish what is wrong – the cause is often an incorrectly-set switch on the control panel, but other faults such as short-circuits, loose wires and dirty track are all easy to identify. Surprisingly, simple automation, such as branch line shuttles, is easy to implement using readily available modules. However, there are disadvantages too.

With DC it is difficult to add operational features to locomotives and rolling stock such as lights. For example, a locomotive factory-fitted with head and tail lights will only operate when power is applied to the track through the controller, which isn't entirely realistic, and it's the same for tail lights too.

The more complicated a layout gets, the more complex – and expensive – the wiring becomes and this comes down, partly, to individual builder's skill levels with wiring and a lot of patience.

While simple automation is possible, complex automation – such as operating main lines automatically whilst shunting a goods yard – is difficult to implement and inflexible, but DC control can also provide a lot of 'building' pleasure as a layout develops – particularly when the finished project works.

Pros and cons – DCC

The biggest single advantage of DCC is the ability to park a locomotive anywhere on a layout, even right next to another locomotive, without the need for isolating sections. This mimics the way the real railway operates as even when there is a large amount of spare siding space, locomotives tend to 'huddle' together.

This is achieved through the controller which communicates with a decoder inside a locomotive, rather than the rails, to increase and decrease speed (voltage) and control additional functions such as lights and sounds.

Regardless of the complexity of the layout, with DCC the wiring remains substantially the same and straightforward, although for very large layouts additional boosters or power districts may be required for the best running qualities which is where life gets a little more complex.

DCC operation is no longer constrained by electrical sections and, if you desire, an entire layout can be built without the need to install a single switch. For example at a real terminus an arriving train engine follows the departing coaches out to the end of the platform so that the signalman doesn't forget about it. This is easy to replicate with DCC without worrying about switches or electrical sections.

Model performance can also be tailored using DCC through the decoder which has a multitude of settings which can be adjusted to personal tastes. By configuring the decoder, the start voltage, maximum speed, acceleration rate and many other values can be altered.

Unlike DC, complex automation can be implemented, albeit at a price, but once installed it can easily be changed to suit differing circumstances. However, simple automation, such as branch line shuttles, is more complicated to implement with DCC.

There are however, disadvantages of DCC too. Equipment, whether it's a factory fitted DCC locomotive, a controller or a decoder, costs more than conventional DC equipment. Each locomotive needs its own decoder and some people will choose to have these fitted for them. If you intend to convert a large collection of locomotives the cost could be prohibitive – between £10 and £20 per decoder per locomotive.

It can also be difficult to fit decoders in locomotives – even DCC ready ones can prove tricky at times – because of a lack of space or simply because the body is awkward to remove from the chassis.

Fault finding is more complex too as DCC relies on invisible signals which are transmitted through electrical wires. When things don't work the fault can lie in a number of places and it needs a logical approach to tie the problem down. It can be as simple as using the wrong locomotive address or as complicated as a malfunctioning decoder or track feeds that are not up to the job.

The process of configuring decoders can be tedious. To get the best out of each locomotive you need to set various parameters such as starting voltage and maximum speed. This requires a fair bit of trial and error and, more importantly, time. Fortunately it only has to be done once and, to be honest, many people never bother to do it at all.

DCC myths and misconceptions

■ **It's expensive.** Well, yes it is if you are trying to convert a medium or large layout and matching locomotive stud all at once. It would be far better to phase DCC operation in or, if you really must do it all at once, save up for it.

■ **The decoders are difficult to fit.** They can be. Small locomotives, such as 'N' scale saddle-tanks can be difficult. Vintage commercial products with live metal chassis can also cause problems, as can kit and scratchbuilt steam locomotives but in many cases there is a workaround. There are very few models where it really is impossible to fit a DCC decoder.

■ **DCC won't work with certain types of point.** Simply not true. DCC is more sensitive to short circuits so if you have a problem with incorrectly wired or built points or wildly out of gauge wheelsets that cause a short going over pointwork, then DCC will highlight the problem. The fault lies with the wiring or wheels and ought to be corrected anyway.

■ **DCC needs special wiring.** Not true. Whilst you may wish to put special wiring in you can replace a conventional controller on your layout with a DCC one and it will work as long as you don't have any high frequency track cleaners or lighting installed.

■ **DCC needs programming.** Programming is a bad choice of word. As a minimum all you need to do is set the decoder's number in each locomotive. This is usually a matter of a few key presses. That's it. You don't need to know, adjust or program anything else. Setting a video recorder is harder.

■ **DCC isn't needed on a small layout.** DCC is ideally suited to small layouts. The ability to stop a locomotive anywhere, regardless of dead sections, is a boon to operators of compact layouts. If you had a small layout depicting a motive power depot you could park locomotives nose to tail in prototypical fashion. You could also operate the points and signals from your handheld controller rather than a control panel.

■ **DCC isn't needed on a large layout.** DCC is ideally suited to large layouts too. The ability to select any locomotive and then run it without having to worry about setting section switches, reverse loops and isolating sections means that you can concentrate on driving the train.

■ **You need to buy a special tester.** Like most technological gadgets offered to consumers, DCC items work when you take them out of the box. In the unlikely event that they don't – take them back to the retailer.

■ **You need a computer to get the best out of DCC.** You can link DCC up to a computer if you wish. The computer can work some, or all, of your layout, but it doesn't have to.

Common problems

With any model railway control system there are factors which need to be considered and flaws which need to be addressed. Whichever system you use you still need to ensure that electricity can get to every track. You will also need to ensure that there are no sections that are, or can

Locomotives factory fitted with digital sound are becoming more common from Bachmann and Hornby is also introducing sound fitted locomotives in 2008. However, there are kits available to equip other locomotives with sound chips such as this set-up from South West Digital. Ian Morton.

unexpectedly become, electrically dead and live frog points need special treatment.

The better the equipment you buy, the better it will perform. This applies to DCC decoders as much as DC controllers. A cheap DCC decoder, which is in effect the locomotive's own controller, will not give you the same level of performance as a more expensive model.

The same is true of DC controllers – whilst a train set controller will do the job you will get far better results from a more advanced design, even if they do look much the same.

Although it may seem odd, the choice between DCC and DC might also be forced by your choice of period too. At the moment there are more DCC functions available to the diesel traction

modeller – working lights and sounds – whereas steam locomotives tend to benefit from the ability to customise their performance. That said, both Hornby and Bachmann are due to release their first DCC sound fitted steam locomotives in 2008, a 'Duchess' and 'Jubilee' respectively, which may sway a few more DCC followers. Equally, there are DCC sound chips for other steam

Taking the pain out of chip installation – the Bachmann 'Jubilee' 4-6-0

Step 1

Some shy away from Digital Command Control (DCC) because of the fear of decoder installation, but it doesn't have to be difficult. Admittedly, some locomotives are more complex than others, but, generally, the newer the model, the simpler chip fitting will be. This DCC ready Bachmann 'Jubilee' is a straightforward case which requires only a small crosshead screwdriver and a pair of tweezers to fit a decoder.

Step 2

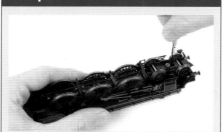

The first task is to remove the two body securing screws from the chassis. One is located at the rear of the chassis and secures the tender drawbar and the other is located under the front bogie. Conveniently, Bachmann has put a hole through the front bogie directly below the screw for access. The screws are small, so make sure you keep them (and the tender drawbar) safe ready for reassembly.

Step 3

Next, gently ease the body off the chassis. This is usually fairly easy, but do take care when handling steam locomotive chassis as there are many components which are easy to distort. Diesel locomotives are easier to work with from this point of view. Keep the chassis on a solid work bench whilst removing the body as this reduces the risk of dropping it and damaging it.

locomotives available from other suppliers, including South West Digital, but they do require a little skill to install.

It's difficult to state that you should use either one of the two types of control currently available, as it really depends on your skills, budget, desires and whether you already have an operating model railway – starting from scratch with DCC is much easier than converting an existing fleet and layout. If realistic railway operation is what you want, DCC may be the way to go, although you can achieve a lot with DC control too.

Our advice is to weigh up the options set out here, talk to users of each system and, if you can, try out different products to assess which suits you best.

DCC – a bright future...
Digital Command Control is an extensive subject and in future issues of *Hornby Magazine* we will be looking into more of the do's and don'ts, and bringing you tips and techniques on how to make the best of this system.

As with any product involving digital technology – like computers and cameras – the rate of development is rapid and new control systems are being developed to increase the potential of DCC.

DCC product manufacturers

There is a wide range of products available for DCC. These are the main DCC control manufacturers together with their website addresses.

Each company has its own design of system which complies with the NMRA standards. Visit the websites to find out more about the individual systems or talk to your local model railway shop.

■ **Bachmann**	www.bachmann.co.uk
■ **Digitrax**	www.digitrax.com
■ **ESU**	www.loksound.de
■ **Gaugemaster**	www.gaugemaster.com
■ **Hornby**	www.hornby.com
■ **Lenz Digital Plus**	www.lenz.com
■ **NCE**	www.ncedcc.com
■ **Zimo**	www.zimo.at

Step 4

When the body is off, this is what you will find. Although there are detail differences between chassis, most steam locomotives look fairly similar, even between manufacturers. The decoder socket is located beneath the green blanking plug on top of the small printed circuit board.

Step 5

The blanking plug, which sets this DCC ready model as an analogue model from the box, is, again, simple to remove. A pair of tweezers is handy for a stubborn blanking plug, but whichever way you remove, do it gently and don't force it, as this could lead to a damaged or snapped leg.

Step 6

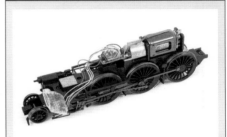

Next, the DCC decoder plug can be inserted into the socket. Before installing, read the instructions supplied both with the locomotive and decoder carefully to establish which is pin one. This is a Bachmann chip. It is then simply a case of plugging the decoder plug into the socket on the chassis.

Step 7

Many ready-to-run DCC ready steam locomotives have a specially designed pocket to locate a DCC decoder chip. The Bachmann 'Jubilee' has a dedicated area in the front of the boiler and the chip can simply be slotted in before the body is replaced on the chassis. It is worth testing the chip installation at this stage before re-fitting the body.

Step 8

Carefully re-assemble the chassis taking care to ensure that none of the wires from the decoder chip snag or foul the bodywork on the way back in. Gently push the chassis back into place, once home re-fit the screws – tweezers are very useful for placing the screws back in position – then re-tighten using a small crosshead screwdriver.

Step 9

That's all there is to it. The final job is to re-test the installation before configuring the chip. From the factory all chips are pre-set to address '0003', so to fit in with your locomotive fleet it may be necessary to re-address the chip. Other than that, this 'Jubilee' is ready for action on a DCC layout.

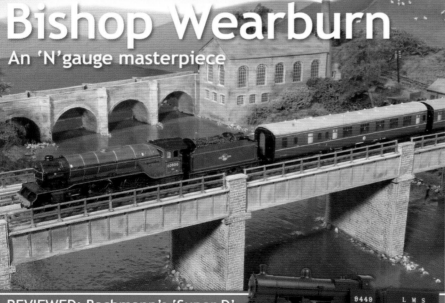

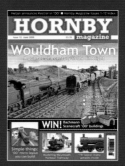

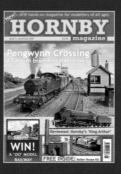
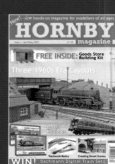